Eyewitness

GREAT SCIENTISTS

Charles Babbage's Difference Engine No. 1

Hubble space telescope

Section of the DNA double helix model

Nanorobot examines the inner wall of a blood vessel

Astrolabe

C. Darwin

Charles Darwin's compass

Falling
feather

Eyewitness
GREAT
SCIENTISTS

Written by
JACQUELINE FORTEY

Botanical
collections

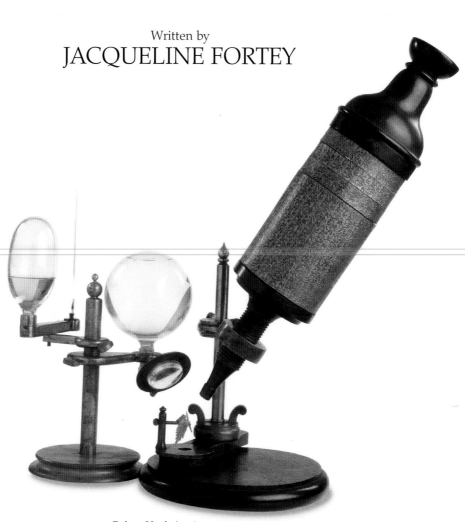

Robert Hooke's microscope

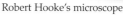

DK Publishing, Inc.

Newton's
apples

South American
butterflies

Archimedes'
screw

LONDON, NEW YORK,
MUNICH, MELBOURNE, AND DELHI

Consultant Dr. Patricia Fara

Managing editor Camilla Hallinan
Managing art editor Martin Wilson
Publishing manager Sunita Gahir
Category publisher Andrea Pinnington
DK picture library Claire Bowers
Senior art editor David Ball
Production Angela Graef
DTP designers Andy Hilliard, Siu Ho, Ben Hung
Jacket designer Andy Smith

For Cooling Brown Ltd
Creative director Arthur Brown
Editor Jemima Dunne
Designers Juliette Norsworthy, Tish Jones
Picture researcher Louise Thomas

First published in the United States in 2007
by DK Publishing
375 Hudson Street
New York, New York 10014

07 08 09 10 11 10 9 8 7 6 5 4 3 2 1
ED494 – 04/07

DK books are available at special discounts when purchased in bulk for
sales promotions, premiums, fundraising, or educational use. For details, contact:
DK Publishing Special Markets
375 Hudson Street
New York, New York 10014
SpecialSales@dk.com

A catalog record for this book is available from
the Library of Congress.

ISBN: 978-0-7566-2974-8 (HC)
978-0-7566-2973-1 (Library Binding)

Color reproduction by Colourscan, Singapore
Printed and bound in China by Toppan Printing Co. (Shenzen) Ltd

Discover more at
www.dk.com

Galileo's
pendulum clock

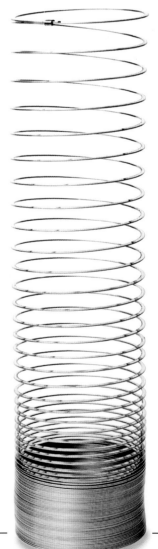

Hooke's law

Contents

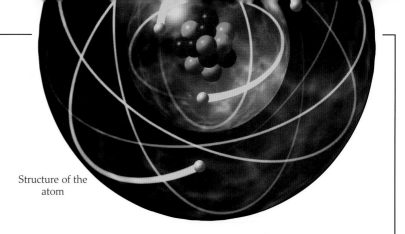

Structure of the atom

Aristotle

ARISTOTLE (C. 384–322 BCE)
This portrait shows how 15th-century Dutch artist Joos van Gent thought the philosopher looked. Aristotle's ideas about an ordered universe appealed to the Christian Church and became so central to its teaching that it was difficult for later scholars to challenge the theories.

I N 387 BCE, THE FAMOUS PHILOSOPHER Plato set up a new center for learning, called an Academy, in the Greek city of Athens. One of his pupils was Aristotle, a doctor's son from Macedonia, then part of northeastern Greece, who later became tutor to Alexander the Great. Plato valued abstract thought, using reason to arrive at a conclusion and believed the basic units of the universe were five geometric solids, including the tetrahedron (a solid with four faces) and the cube. Aristotle was interested in what could be learned directly from the physical world. He classified knowledge into different fields, and wrote a book, *Physics*, that described how nature should be studied. Aristotle looked at objects as well as living things to see how they relate to each other and form part of a larger order.

Stone falls with little or no resistance to air

384 BCE	*Aristotle born in Stagira, Chalcidice, in southeastern Macedonia, then part of Greece.*
367 BCE	*Joins Plato's Academy in Athens, remaining a pupil there until the age of 37.*
C. 350 BCE	*Writes* On the Parts of Animals, *and other works on animals, establishing an area of science later called biology. Also writes* Physics, *explaining his ideas about natural philosophy.*
347 BCE	*Leaves the Academy (and Athens) when Plato dies.*
C. 342 BCE	*Invited by King Philip of Macedonia to educate his 13-year-old son, who later became known as Alexander the Great.*
336 BCE	*Arrives at the court of King Philip, where he remains for several years.*
335 BCE	*Returns to Athens and founds his own school of philosophy, the Lyceum. Many of his written works date from his time here.*
323 BCE	*Alexander the Great dies. Macedonians become unpopular in Athens so Aristotle retires to Chalcis, Euboea, second largest of the Greek Aegean islands.*
322 BCE	*Aristotle dies, aged 62, in Chalcis.*
60 BCE	*Aristotle's works first published, by Andronicus of Rhodes.*

Parthenon

CENTER FOR LEARNING
The ruins of the Parthenon look down on the Greek city of Athens. This temple was begun in 447 BCE by the politician Pericles, to demonstrate the power and wealth of the Athenian Empire. The city became a magnet for the arts and learning, especially for scholars known as philosophers, who spent time thinking about the world and how to understand it.

WALKING AND TALKING
Aristotle is often depicted in Renaissance religious paintings. In the Vatican in Rome, Italy, this magnificent 16th-century fresco (wall painting) by Raphael celebrates classical learning. Aristotle and his teacher Plato are in the center, surrounded by philosophers. Plato is pointing upward to the heavens, and Aristotle's downward gesture reflects his interest in the Earth. Aristotle studied in Plato's Academy for 20 years. In 335 BCE Aristotle set up his own Lyceum in Athens, where students discussed ideas as they strolled through covered walkways, called *peripatoi*. His followers became known as peripatetics.

School of Athens by Raphael, in the Stanza della Segnatura, Vatican, 1505–11 CE

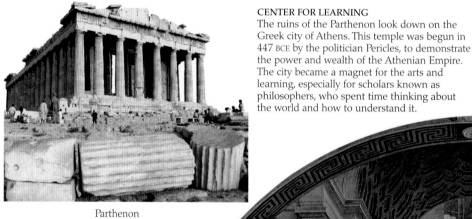

FALLING OBJECTS

In Aristotle's view, everything on Earth was made of a combination of four elements: earth, fire, water, and air. A stone (mostly earth), is pulled back down to Earth, wheras smoke (mostly air) rises upward. The speed at which objects fall, he said, is proportional to their weight, so heavier objects fall faster. When comparing a falling stone with something as light as a falling feather, this appears to be true, because air resistance slows the feather down. In fact, without this resistance, objects fall at the same rate, as Galileo (pp. 16–17) proved nearly 2,000 years later.

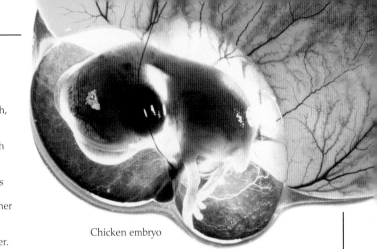

Chicken embryo

LOOKING AT ANIMALS

Aristotle encouraged the study of the physical world, particularly living things. He made detailed descriptions of animals, dissected 50 species, and wrote about animal movement and reproduction. Among his observations was a precise account of the development of a chicken embryo. When Aristotle looked at animals (and objects), he considered four "causes." He would ask himself "What is it made of? What is its form or essence? How did it come into being? For what purpose?" This helped him to classify animals into groups.

CRYSTAL SPHERES

Aristotle thought that the universe consisted of transparent spheres revolving one inside another, kept in motion around a fixed Earth by an outer sphere called the Prime Mover. This idea of Earth and space with everything in its place did not change until the mid 16th century. The diagram shows the Earth at the center, made up of four elements (earth, fire, air, and water), with spheres carrying the Sun, Moon, six planets, and the stars.

Prime mover, shown here as Christian God

Fire

Air

Water and earth

Feather appears to fall more slowly, because of air resistance

Moon sphere

Sun sphere

Spheres for planets Saturn, Jupiter, Mars, Venus, and Mercury, with their symbols

Heavenly sphere with fixed stars and astrological symbols

Earth-centered universe, 1539, based on the ideas of Aristotle and Claudius Ptolemy (C. 85–165 CE)

> *"Wisdom is the knowledge about principles and causes."*
>
> **ARISTOTLE**
> Metaphysics C. 350 BCE

THE FOUR HUMORS

Greek scholars believed that the four elements that made up all matter on the Earth were also linked to human character, bodily fluids, and seasonal variations, in the four humors. Phlegm stood for a calm personality, winter (cold and moist), and water. Sanguine (blood) was linked with a cheerful character, spring (hot and moist), and air. Choleric (yellow bile) was for active people, summer (hot and dry), and fire. Melancholic was linked with black bile, a depressive temperament, the fall (cold and dry), and earth. To be healthy, a person's humors had to be balanced.

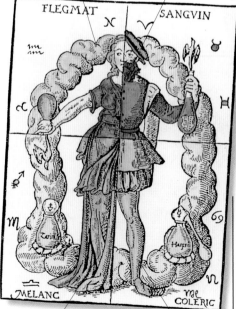

Phlegm, or phlegmatic

Sanguine

FLEGMAT SANGVIN

MELANC mc COLERIC

Melancholic

Choleric

16th-century engraving of the humors

Archimedes

FOR CENTURIES, A MEDIEVAL MANUSCRIPT now in the Walter Art Museum, Baltimore, USA, concealed writings by the mathematical genius, Archimedes. The paintings on the pages of the manuscript have been scraped off and the parchments scanned with X-rays, revealing the only known copy of his treatise about buoyancy, *On Floating Bodies*, in the original Greek. Archimedes valued his mathematical achievements most, in particular working out the ratio of a cylinder's volume to that of a sphere. Archimedes also used math to explain the principles behind levers, pulleys, and other important aspects of the physical world. He was a skillful engineer, designing machines to lift water and heavy loads with relatively little effort, and was frequently called on to solve problems by the king of his native city-state, Syracuse, in Sicily.

ARCHIMEDES (287–212 BCE)
This 18th-century portrait of Archimedes by Giuseppe Nogari shows him as an elderly man, holding a pair of dividers. Accounts about his life were written long after he died, and it is difficult to tell fact from fiction, because there are many legends about him.

287 BCE	Archimedes born in Syracuse, on the island of Sicily (now in Italy), the son of Phidias, an astronomer.
275 BCE	Military takeover of the city-state Syracuse by King Hiero II, a close friend or relative of Archimedes.
C. 265 BCE	Solves the problem of calculating the gold content of Hiero's crown, after observing the effect of water displacement in his bathtub.
C. 269 BCE	Believed to have studied in Alexandria, Egypt, in the school of the Greek mathematician, Euclid. May have invented the hydraulic screw here.
C. 263 BCE	Returns to Syracuse, for the rest of his life. Develops many major theories here, including principles of mechanics and buoyancy, and methods for finding the surface and volume of geometrical objects.
C. 215 BCE	Hiero II of Syracuse dies and is succeeded by his 15-year-old grandson, Hieronymous, who is assassinated about a year later.
213 BCE	Syracuse besieged by the Romans under Marcus Claudius Marcellus.
212 BCE	Dies during the Roman invasion.

ALEXANDRIA
A city founded by Alexander the Great in 313 BCE on the coast of Egypt became a new center of Greek commerce and learning. As a student in Alexandria, Archimedes is believed to have studied with another outstanding mathematician, Euclid (C. 325–265 BCE), who compiled a famous book on geometry called *Elements*.

Irrigation channel at higher level

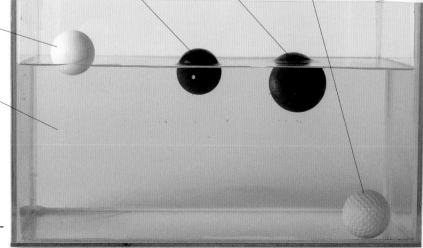

Denser squash ball displaces (pushes aside) more water than table-tennis ball

Solid hardwood ball sinks until it is almost submerged

Heavy golf ball sinks

Light table-tennis ball floats high in the water

Water's density (weight per unit of volume) is less than that of the golf ball

ARCHIMEDES' PRINCIPLE
Here three balls float in a tank, but at different levels in the water, and a fourth ball has sunk to the bottom. This is because an object sinks until it has pushed aside an amount of liquid that is equal to its weight, unless it is more dense than the liquid, in which case it sinks. Archimedes calculated that floating objects are supported by an upward force, called buoyancy, that equals the weight of liquid they displace.

Colored engraving of Archimedes in his bathtub, 1547

CROWN VALUE

A famous story was told by the Roman architect Vitruvius. Archimedes was asked to find out whether King Hiero II's new crown was made of a metal less valuable than gold. As he stepped into a full bathtub, the water overflowed. He sprang out of the bath and ran home naked, shouting "Eureka!" His body had displaced an equal amount of water, and he applied the same principle to measuring the crown. A gold crown would displace less water than one made from a mixture of gold and the heavier metal, silver.

"Eureka!"
(I've found it!)

ARCHIMEDES
told by Vitruvius Pollio, 1st century BCE

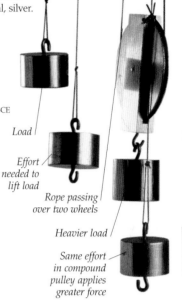

Load

Effort needed to lift load

Rope passing over two wheels

Heavier load

Same effort in compound pulley applies greater force

COMPOUND PULLEYS

"Give me a place to stand and I will move the Earth", is a much-quoted remark by Archimedes. Hiero II asked him to prove this by designing a machine that could move a heavy ship. Archimedes devised a set of pulleys, with a rope passing over grooved wheels. This magnifies the force applied when a rope at the end is pulled because the rope moves up more slowly than the weight. This force, known as effort, is represented here by the hooked weights on these pulleys. The effort (pulley weight) is the same in each of the examples, but the force increases with the number of turns of the rope around the wheels.

Turning handle requires a small amount of effort to lift a heavy load

Water flows out of tube into irrigation channel

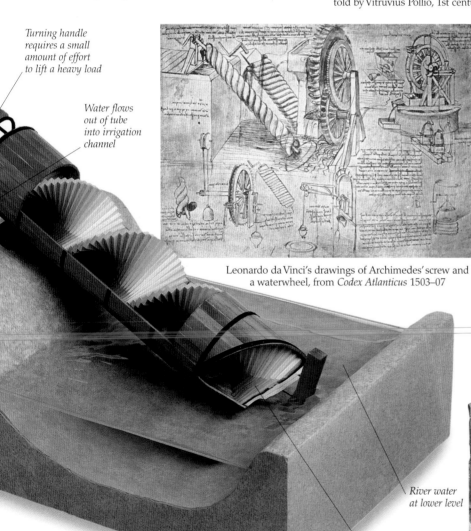

Leonardo da Vinci's drawings of Archimedes' screw and a waterwheel, from *Codex Atlanticus* 1503–07

River water at lower level

Cutaway model of Archimedes' screw, used for irrigation

Sloping blades scoop up water as they turn

THE HYDRAULIC SCREW

Archimedes designed this ingenious device for lifting water to higher levels, such as river water to irrigate crops, or to pump water out of ships. It is still used today. The screw consists of a spiral shaft with sloping blades enclosed within a tube. The tube is placed at an angle with the lower end in the water. When a handle at the top of the shaft is turned, the blades rotate, scooping up water at the bottom and carrying it upward. The later versions in the drawing by Renaissance artist and inventor Leonardo da Vinci (1452–1519) show spiral tubes wrapped around a shaft.

THE SIEGE OF SYRACUSE

Roman warships powered by banks of rowers, seen here in a relief from the 1st century BCE, were a formidable force. When the city of Syracuse was besieged in 212 BCE by Marcellus's fleet, Archimedes' war machines sprang into action. One was a "claw" made from a weighted pole, operated by pulleys and levers, with an iron grappling hook that could grasp and upend enemy ships.

Zhang Heng

CHINA IN THE SECOND CENTURY CE led the world in many areas of science and technology. Inexpensive paper, accurate water clocks, sundials, the compass, movable type, gunpowder, and medical techniques such as acupuncture were all in use in China long before they appeared elsewhere. The astronomer and mathematician Zhang Heng was a highly principled and versatile official at the Han emperor's court. He applied the first grid system to maps, studied lunar eclipses, and charted 2,500 stars with the help of a moving celestial sphere. Zhang Heng also designed an odometer, (a wheeled device for measuring distances) and an earthquake warning system.

ZHANG HENG (78–139 CE)
This porcelain statue of Zhang Heng shows him in flowing robes and holding a golden celestial sphere. An accomplished painter, writer, and poet, he became interested in astronomy at about the age of 30. When he became a government official, he campaigned against corruption in the civil service.

CHINESE PAPERMAKING
Sheets of paper are hung up to dry in the ancient Chinese art of papermaking. The Han Emperor's secretary Cai Lun (50–121 CE) improved papermaking by introducing plant fibers. Paper was lighter, thinner, and cheaper to produce and replaced silk as a writing material for educated people. This played a vital role in spreading knowledge within China, and later in the Middle East and Europe.

18th-century painting of Chinese papermaking

78	*Zhang Heng (pronounced Chung Hong) born in Shiqiao, near what is now Nanyang, Henan Province, China. Leaves home to study literature and become a writer.*
106	*Eastern Han Emperor, An Di, comes to the throne, ruling from a large palace complex at the capital at Luoyang in Henan Province*
c. 108	*Zhang Heng becomes famous for his poetry and other literary works and begins to study astronomy.*
111	*Works for government, eventually in charge of astronomical observation, astrology, calendars, and weather forecasting.*
123	*Adjusts the Chinese calendar to link more closely with the seasons.*
132	*Designs a device for "measuring seasonal winds and Earth movements," and a water-powered armillary sphere.*
138	*His early-warning system detects an earthquake in Longxi, China.*
139	*Dies at 61; is remembered for prose poems and scientific achievements.*

"The sky is like a hen's egg . . . the Earth is like the yolk of the egg."
ZHANG HENG
in his book on astronomy, *Ling Xiang*

Celestial equator

Celestial meridian

Replica of Zhang Heng's Armillary sphere, 1439

STUDYING THE STARS
Zhang Heng designed the first known armillary sphere to be rotated on its axis by a system of water-powered gears, shown here in a brass replica in Nanjing, China. This is a cutaway model of a huge imaginary celestial sphere around the Earth that is subdivided by a number of interlocking rings. These rings represent imaginary lines, including a celestial equator, and celestial meridians that pass over the north and south poles. They are each marked out with measurements to help astronomers locate stars.

Crescent Moon

First quarter

Waxing

Full Moon

Waning

Last quarter

LUNAR CALENDAR

During each month, the Moon moves through a cycle of changes called phases. A waxing Moon is early in the cycle, and the waning Moon is finishing its cycle. Each cycle is called a lunation, and takes an average of 29.5 days. The months in the traditional Chinese calendar are based on lunations, each beginning with a new Moon, making a total of 354 days in their year. As the Emperor's Minister, Zhang Heng made adjustments to the calendar to make it fit more closely with the seasons.

Eight dragons face in main compass directions

Open-mouthed toad to catch ball

Central pendulum

Set of levers

Reconstruction of Zhang Heng's earthquake detector

EARTHQUAKE DETECTOR

Several serious earthquakes in China prompted Zhang Heng to design an early warning device. Experts are still trying to decide exactly how it worked. In this reconstruction a pendulum moves inside the bronze urn when an earthquake's tremors are felt. This operates a lever that opens a dragon's mouth and a ball drops into the mouth of the toad below it, making a noise to sound the alarm. The empty dragon's mouth indicates the direction of the earthquake. Records say that Zhang Heng's machine detected an earthquake 400 miles (640 km) away.

Cross-section of Zhang Heng's earthquake detector

EXPLOSIVE EXPERIMENTS

During the Han dynasty (206 BCE–220 CE), alchemists (early chemists) began to mix sulfur and saltpeter (postassium nitrate) to discover the secret of life, with explosive results. The combination of these chemicals is now called gunpowder. By 1050 CE, this gunpowder was used to create colorful firework displays for celebrations and by the military to fire arrows and lances.

THE SILK ROAD

In the 13th century, Marco Polo made his world-fabled journey from Venice to China along the Silk Road. This grew from a network of tracks within China into a 5,000-mile (8,000-km) trade route crossing China, central Asia, and India to Europe. Under the Han emperors, traffic along the Silk Road increased, with camel caravans carrying silk, jade, metalwork, and ceramics eastward from China, and bringing gold and luxury foods to China from the West. Scientific advances that may have left China via this route are printing, gunpowder, the astrolabe, and the compass.

Marco Polo's route to and from China (1271–95)

Alhazen

AFTER THE COLLAPSE OF the Roman Empire in 476 CE, Europe lost touch with the learning of the Ancient Greeks, but a golden age dawned in the Middle East. In 762, the city of Baghdad (in present-day Iraq) became capital of a new Islamic, or Muslim, empire, ruled by Abbasid caliphs. Science flourished in academies such as the House of Wisdom, where manuscripts and books from Greece, India, and Persia (now Iran), were translated and studied. Alhazen, from neighboring Basra, excelled at physics, mathematics (especially geometry), medicine, and astronomy. He is often regarded as the founder of the science of optics, as he conducted experiments to investigate reflection and refraction (bending of light), and used mathematics to analyze the results.

ALHAZEN (965–1040)
The seven volumes of Alhazen's *Book of Optics* reveal his methodical way of working. His theories about light were supported by careful studies of its properties. He passed light through lenses and water-filled vessels, bounced it from mirrors, curved and flat, and studied moonlight, eclipses, shadows, and the effects of the setting Sun.

965	*Abu Ali Hasan Ibn al-Haitham, also known as Alhazen, born in Persian city of Basra, now in Iraq. Educated in Basra and Baghdad.*
969	*Fatimid caliphs (Islamic leaders) conquer the Nile valley and found the city of Cairo, Egypt.*
975	*Al-Hakim becomes caliph of Egypt. He is a cruel ruler, but a patron of scientific learning.*
c. 1000	*Alhazen writes works on optics, astronomy, and mathematics.*
c. 1015	*Goes to Egypt at the request of caliph Al-Hakim to regulate the flow of water in the Nile, a task that proves impossible.*
c. 1020	*Philosopher Ibn Sina (Avicenna) writes his great scientific works,* The Book of Healing *and* The Canon of Medicine.
1021	*Al-Hakim dies. Some reports say Alhazen went to Spain to study, others say he remained in Egypt.*
1027	*Gives up being a civil servant to devote himself to scientific study.*
1040	*Dies, possibly in Egypt.*
1270	*His huge work* Book of Optics *is translated into Latin as* Opticae Thesaurus Alhazeni, *and influences scholars in Europe, including Roger Bacon.*

ASTRONOMICAL COMPUTER
Arabic astronomers perfected the astrolabe, an invaluable instrument used in the Middle Ages to measure the heights of stars, tell the time by day or night, and make a host of other calculations. The universe is shown with the Earth at its center. This brass example has a base plate with a sky map, and a movable "dial" with pointers representing fixed stars.

Star map, or rete, can be rotated

Egyptian astrolabe c. 1100

Base plate with lines for calculation

Page from 14th-century version of Avicenna's *The Canon of Medicine*

Arabic calligraphy on vellum

ISLAMIC MANUSCRIPTS
Prized manuscripts written on vellum or on paper provided a invaluable storehouse of information for scholars. The text from this Persian medical book was hand-lettered onto vellum and illustrated with miniature paintings. Islamic scholars like Alhazen read, copied, and translated many Greek texts, often adding comments.

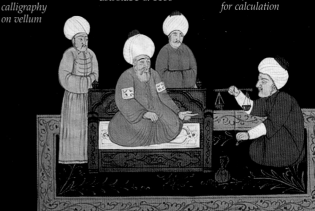

In this 17th century Ottoman (Turkish) illustration from *Treaty of Medicine*, Avicenna is seated with scales

ADVANCED MEDICINE
Alhazen's contemporary, Persian philospher Ibn Sina, also called Avicenna (980–1037), is shown teaching his pupils how to prepare a remedy for smallpox. His encyclopaedia *The Canon of Medicine* combines the expertise of Greek scholars, such as Galen, and of Islamic physicians. It defines medicine as the art of conserving health and restoring it when it is lost, and identifies the elements— earth, air, fire, and water—as the body's building blocks

CITY OF CAIRO

Cairo's great mosque was begun just after the city was founded in 969, and became the center of one of the world's oldest universities. Alhazen probably spent some years here teaching, writing, and copying manuscripts. Accounts say that he was invited to Egypt by Caliph Al-Hakim to help regulate the flow of water on the Nile River. When the project failed, he feared for his life. Al-Hakim had an erratic temper, so Alhazen pretended to be insane until the caliph died.

Al-Azhar mosque, Cairo, Egypt

Muscle moves eyeball

Tear gland

INSIDE THE EYE

Some early scholars believed that eyes gave out rays of light. Alhazen used experiments to test this "emission" theory, and proved that light enters the eye, bringing information with it. He gave the first accurate description of the eye's different parts, and explained how the brain and the eye work together to give us sight. Light enters the eye, is refracted by the cornea through the pupil, and then passes through the lens onto the retina. From there information provided by light travels as impulses along the optic nerve to the brain.

Optic nerve carries information from retina to brain

TWILIGHT

As the Sun sinks below the horizon, the point where the sky and earth seem to meet, it continues to give out a glow. Alhazen made a detailed study of light and the thickness of the atmosphere, and calculated that twilight only ends when the Sun is about 19 degrees below the horizon. He showed that it is caused by light refraction (the bending of light as it moves through materials of different densities) in the atmosphere.

Front of eye is cornea, colored part behind it is iris, pupil is central hole

Lens

Skull

Eyeball

"It is not a ray that leaves the eye and meets the object that gives rise to vision."

ALHAZEN
in his *Book of Optics*, 11th century

Diagram of the human eye, from Alhazen's *Opticae Thesaurus*, first published in 1572

MOORISH SPAIN

The arches and columns inside this famous building in Córdoba are examples of the decorative arts of southern Spain under Moorish, or Muslim, rule (711–1402). Built as a mosque, it is now a Catholic church. From 929 to 1236, Córdoba was capital of an Islamic empire that stretched to northwest Africa. It was the most advanced city in medieval Europe. With a large population and many palaces and libraries, scientific scholarship flourished in an atmosphere of religious tolerance. From Muslim Spain, knowledge and ideas filtered to Christian northern Europe.

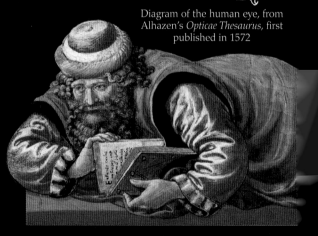

The Mesquita, Córdoba

CÓRDOBA'S COMMENTATOR

Córdoban philosopher Ibn Rushd, also called Averroes (1126–98), reawakened European interest in Aristotle by writing interpretations of his work. Averroes was an expert in mathematics, medicine, and law, and believed that religion and reason need not conflict. This portrait of Averroes in a painting by Benozzo Gozzoli (1471) shows that his ideas were still being debated long after his death.

Roger Bacon

ROGER BACON (c. 1214–92)
This picture of Bacon, painted long after he died, shows him wearing a friar's robes. When in the Franciscan monastery, he was isolated from other scholars because of his views. However, Bacon earned the respect of later generations of scientists for his advanced ideas.

THE NAME "DOCTOR MIRABILIS," meaning wonderful teacher, was a nickname given to the medieval philosopher, Roger Bacon. He was fiery, hardworking, and an ardent seeker for the truth, at a time when Europe was still behind the Arab world in scientific scholarship. In the 13th century, few people were educated, aside from those working in the church. After teaching the works of Aristotle at the universities of Paris and Oxford, Bacon became a Franciscan friar. He gathered all his ideas about mathematics, physics, grammar, and philosophy into a huge book, *Opus Majus*, which he then sent to his supporter Pope Clement IV in Rome. But his efforts were in vain, since the pope died before he could read this extraordinary compendium. Bacon was eventually imprisoned by the Franciscan order for his outspoken views.

MONASTIC LIFE
A Franciscan monk sits at his desk in a writing room called a scriptorium. Bacon had intended to continue the study of science and languages, when he joined a Franciscan monastery in Oxford in 1253. He was convinced that finding out about the natural world was essential to understanding God. However, this was against Franciscan teaching, and because of his views, he was sent to Paris, where he was forbidden to continue his research. Undaunted, he set about reforming the Christian calendar.

c. 1214	Born, probably in Ilchester in Somerset, England, into a land-owning family.
1227	Goes to Oxford University, England, aged 13. Becomes a master and lectures there on Aristotle until 1241.
1241	Travels to France to teach at the University of Paris, the center of European intellectual life at the time.
1247	Returns to Oxford, where he buys books and instruments, and devotes himself entirely to his studies and teaching.
c. 1253	Joins the Franciscan Order of Friars Minor, Oxford.
1256	Sent to a monastery in Paris—isolated from other scholars, he works on calendar reform.
1266	Sends a letter to Pope Clement IV suggesting improvements to the curriculum.
1267	Compiles and sends a summary of his encyclopaedic work, Opus Majus (Great Work), to Pope Clement IV.
1268	Sends further books, Opus Minus (Lesser Work) and Opus Tertium (Third Work) to Rome, but the pope dies in the same year.
1278	Believed to have been imprisoned by the Franciscan order in Ancona, Italy, for 10 years.
1292	Dies in Oxford, England.

REVIVAL IN LEARNING
The Spanish town of Toledo was captured by Muslim Arabs in 712 and later became an important Moorish center. When it was recaptured by the Spanish in 1085, Moorish manuscripts were collected in a great library and translation school, founded by Archbishop Raymund. European scholars, starved for new ideas, flocked to study and translate important works of science and philosophy from Arabic, including books by Greeks such as Aristotle, that had been lost in Europe.

Glass vessel called a retort used for distillation

Alchemical apparatus

Oil heated by flame below

Hourglass with sand to measure time

Bottle for mineral samples

FASCINATED BY LIGHT AND LENSES

This diagram, drawn by Bacon or his teacher, Robert Grosseteste (c. 1170–1253), shows a beam of light refracting (changing direction) as it passes through a glass container full of water. Inspired by Alhazen (pp. 12–13), Bacon became interested in optics (the properties of light and how it interacts with matter). He looked at the effects of mirrors and magnifying lenses and showed light forming a rainbow through glass beads to his students.

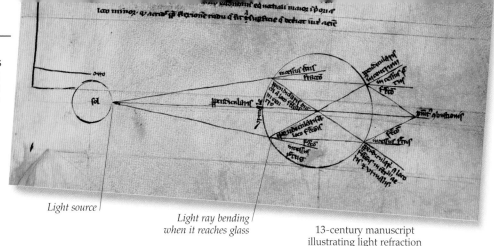

Light source

Light ray bending when it reaches glass

13-century manuscript illustrating light refraction

TESTING BY EXPERIMENT

At a time when many scholars merely accepted past learning without question, Bacon argued that ideas should not be accepted without being tested. A man can be told that fire burns, Bacon said, but he needs to experience the effects of burning, by putting something into the fire, to be convinced that he has been told the truth.

Wood changed to smoke and ash by burning in fire

"Experimental science is the queen of knowledge..."

ROGER BACON
Opus Tertium, 1267

CHURCH CALENDAR

In medieval Europe, the Church calendar and the changing seasons governed people's lives. Each month had its particular tasks, and Christian duties were strictly observed. This 15th-century French manuscript shows the month of March, with peasants tending the fields, and a congregation being blessed in church. However, the Christian calendar was inaccurately calculated, and some time was lost over a year. Bacon argued for its reform, but change did not come until 300 years later.

ALCHEMICAL EXPERIMENTS

These glass containers resembling modern laboratory equipment were used for distillation in alchemy, an early form of chemistry that spread from Alexandria in Egypt to Europe in the Middle Ages. Alchemists experimented on materials, often trying to change one substance into another, such as lead into gold. Bacon was interested in alchemy and astrology, the study of how stars influence daily life. Both of these disciplines had a spiritual side that would not be regarded as a science today.

Hours of Burgundy by unknown 15th-century Flemish artist

Moving dial with signs of the zodiac

Moving dial with Sun and Moon

Twenty four hour face

Oil vapor condenses here

Distillation flask filled with oil

Mortar and pestle for grinding

Test tubes for keeping samples

Stopper with funnel

Crystal ball used to make predictions

Clock in Prague, Czech Republic 1410

MECHANICAL TIME

Magnificent astronomical clocks made in several parts of Europe reveal medieval ideas about a well-ordered universe, with the Earth at its center. On this example, moving dials show the Sun and Moon positions as well as the signs of the zodiac, and the Earth is a flat stationary disk behind them. Richard of Wallingford (1292–1336) designed the earliest of these astronomical devices for St. Alban's Abbey, Hertfordsire, England.

Galileo Galilei

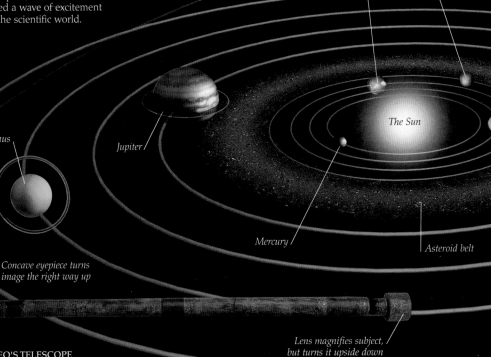

THE ITALIAN MATHEMATICIAN Galileo Galilei made outstanding advances not only in the fields of mathematics, but also in physics and astronomy. He lived at a time when Italy's powerful city-states were at the center of a revival in learning in Europe, and when new ideas could be spread quickly by printed books. Impressed by the work of Archimedes (pp. 8–9), Galileo used mathematics instead of logic to work out problems. His belief in the importance of collecting evidence to support a theory marked a turning point in the way scientists worked. He conducted experiments with moving objects to prove new laws of physics. Among his numerous mechanical inventions was a powerful telescope that began to reveal the secrets of the solar system. However, for Galileo, challenging existing ideas came at a price and brought him into conflict with the Catholic Church.

LAW OF FALLING BODIES
A famous legend describes Galileo dropping objects from the top of Pisa's leaning tower to prove that objects of different weights and sizes fall to the ground at the same speed. It is likely that others carried out this experiment to prove his theory wrong. Based on similar evidence, Galileo's law of falling bodies (1604) did disprove some of the ideas of the Greek thinker Aristotle.

GALILEO GALILEI (1564–1642)
Although his father, a court musician, wanted Galileo to become a doctor, he changed to mathematics. This was the first step in a remarkable scientific career.

1564	*February 15, born in Pisa, Italy, first of six, possibly seven, children.*
1589	*Appointed chair of mathematics at the University of Pisa.*
1592	*Becomes professor of mathematics at the University of Padua in the Republic of Venice, lecturing in geometry and astronomy.*
1595	*Develops an explanation of tides based on the motions of the Earth.*
1602	*Begins to experiment with the pendulum.*
1604	*Begins to experiment with his theory of accelerated motion, which leads to his law of falling bodies. Observes a new star (supernova) for the first time.*
1606	*Designs the thermoscope.*
1609	*Builds a telescope and begins to study the night sky. Makes his first observations of the Moon.*
1610	*Discovers Jupiter's largest moons. Observes that Venus exhibits a full set of phases similar to the Moon. Observes Saturn for first time.*
1616	*Cardinals of the Inquisition forbid Galileo to hold Copernican views.*
1624	*Assured by Pope Urban VII that he can write about his new ideas.*
1632	*Publication of* Dialogue Concerning the Two Chief Systems of the World — *Ptolemaic and Copernican.*
1633	*Placed under house arrest.*
1642	*Dies at his villa in Arcetri.*

THE SOLAR SYSTEM
We know now that the planets move in stately orbits (circular patterns) around the Sun. In Galileo's time, astronomers believed that the Earth's position was fixed, at the center of a vast transparent sphere, across which other heavenly bodies moved. In 1543, a book by Nicolaus Copernicus (1473–1543) placed the Sun firmly in the center of the universe. Galileo was the first person to produce scientific evidence for Copernicus's theory. His revelations about the planet Jupiter, the Moon, and the Sun produced a wave of excitement across the scientific world.

Earth   Mars   Venus

The Sun

Uranus

Jupiter

Mercury

Asteroid belt

Concave eyepiece turns image the right way up

Lens magnifies subject, but turns it upside down

GALILEO'S TELESCOPE
Excited by news of a Flemish spyglass, Galileo built a version of his own that provided greater magnification. The convex lens at the front worked with the concave one in the eyepiece to produce an upright image. By presenting his telescopes to influential patrons, he was able to advance his career as a scientist.

GALILEO'S PENDULUM CLOCK
As a young man, Galileo watched a huge suspended lamp swing to and fro in Pisa cathedral. Timing it with his pulse, he noticed that it took the same amount of time to swing, whatever the length of the swing. Later, when he was designing a clock, he used a swinging pendulum as a mechanism to help it keep accurate time.

The time a pendulum takes to return to its starting position is called a period

Reconstruction of Galileo's clock, 1883

THE INQUISITION AND THE TRIAL OF GALILEO
This 19th-century French painting shows an elderly Galileo standing before a tribunal of the Inquisition in Rome in 1633. In 1616, he received a caution from the Catholic Church for openly supporting the ideas of Copernicus. When a sympathetic cardinal was elected pope in 1624, Galileo felt confident enough to write a new book. This work appeared to defy the Church's earlier ruling and was banned. Penalties for speaking against the Church were severe, so Galileo, already a sick man with failing sight, was sentenced to house arrest in Siena.

Tube filled with liquid

Some globes rise as air inside expands and density changes

GALILEO'S THERMOSCOPE
This is a modern version of the thermoscope—an early thermometer. A sealed tube contains glass globes filled with liquid and air. Each globe has a different density and temperature mark. When the temperature outside changes, the liquid inside the tube expands or contracts, changing its density, which moves the glass globes. The temperature is read from lowest of the upper globes because its density is closest to that of the surrounding liquid.

Each globe contains different amount of air and liquid

GALILEO'S MONUMENT
Despite Galileo's desire to be buried in the splendid family tomb in Santa Croce in Florence, his relatives were worried about displeasing the Church authorities. When his body was finally placed there in 1727, the middle finger of his right hand was removed by an admirer. It can be seen today, encased in a marble and glass stand, in the Museum of the History of Science in Florence.

Pluto (a dwarf planet)

> "I discovered in the heavens many things that had not been seen before our own age."
>
> **GALILEO GALILEI**
> in a letter to Grand Duchess Christina, 1615

High-gain antenna for transmitting data

Saturn

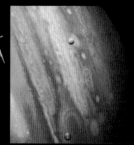

View from the Galileo probe

One of two generators providing power

Galileo Space Probe

Neptune

JUPITER'S MOONS
Galileo's observations showed that Jupiter had its own orbiting moons. In 1610, he wrote a lively description of his discoveries in a book called *The Starry Messenger*, dedicated to the powerful Medici family. Centuries later, a space probe named after Galileo beamed back magnificent images from Jupiter for eight years, until it crash-landed into the planet's surface in 2003.

William Harvey

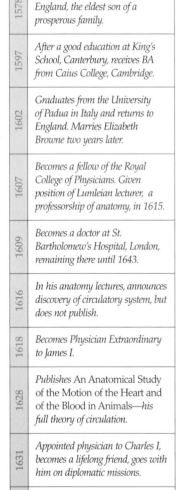

WILLIAM HARVEY (1578–1657)
Seen here looking out of his portrait with an intent gaze, William Harvey was described as a "testy" man, who wore a dagger. The sensitive hands of a skilled anatomist are highlighted against his dark clothing.

1578	*April 1, born in Folkestone, Kent, England, the eldest son of a prosperous family.*
1597	*After a good education at King's School, Canterbury, receives BA from Caius College, Cambridge.*
1602	*Graduates from the University of Padua in Italy and returns to England. Marries Elizabeth Browne two years later.*
1607	*Becomes a fellow of the Royal College of Physicians. Given position of Lumleian lecturer, a professorship of anatomy, in 1615.*
1609	*Becomes a doctor at St. Bartholomew's Hospital, London, remaining there until 1643.*
1616	*In his anatomy lectures, announces discovery of circulatory system, but does not publish.*
1618	*Becomes Physician Extraordinary to James I.*
1628	*Publishes* An Anatomical Study of the Motion of the Heart and of the Blood in Animals—*his full theory of circulation.*
1631	*Appointed physician to Charles I, becomes a lifelong friend, goes with him on diplomatic missions.*
1642	*English Civil War begins. remains with Charles I until the king is beheaded seven years later.*
1651	*Publishes his research on embryology in* Essays on the generation of animals.
1657	*June 3, dies in London. Buried in Hempstead, Essex.*

In 1604, WILLIAM HARVEY married Elizabeth Browne, daughter of the physician to England's Queen Elizabeth I. Already a graduate of the universities of Cambridge, England, and Padua, in Italy, Harvey now had the credentials to establish himself as one of London's leading physicians. He set out on a career as a lecturer, medical practitioner, and royal physician, but it was his research that brought lasting fame. Harvey insisted on testing by observation and experiment rather than accepting traditional ideas. He questioned existing beliefs about the heart and blood, and set out to identify their true function. He published the results in a book that became a cornerstone of modern anatomy.

THE GLADIATORS' DOCTOR
A medieval manuscript of the works of Claudius Galen (129–200 CE) shows a doctor treating a patient. This influential Greek physician attended Roman emperors and was surgeon at a school for gladiators. He made the important discovery that blood, not air, flows through the body's arteries—although he thought it was mixed with pneuma (spirit). Many of his ideas about medical science were unchallenged until the 17th century.

THE ANATOMY THEATRE
This engraving shows Belgian anatomist Andreas Vesalius (1514–64) dissecting a corpse in a crowded church. His seven-volume masterpiece, *On the Fabric of the Human Body*, published in 1543, contains detailed engravings of the interior of the body by Renaissance artists. The book caused a sensation due to the exceptional quality and accuracy of the illustrations.

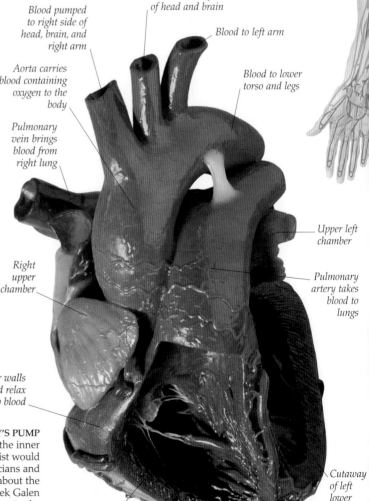

Blood pumped to right side of head, brain, and right arm

Blood to the left side of head and brain

Blood to left arm

Aorta carries blood containing oxygen to the body

Blood to lower torso and legs

Pulmonary vein brings blood from right lung

Right upper chamber

Upper left chamber

Pulmonary artery takes blood to lungs

Muscular walls contract and relax to pump blood

Cutaway of left lower chamber

Cutaway of right lower chamber

Wall dividing right and left chambers of heart

Coronary artery supplies blood to heart muscle

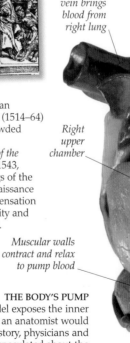

THE BODY'S PUMP
This modern model exposes the inner workings of the heart as an anatomist would see them. Throughout history, physicians and philosophers had speculated about the function of this vital organ. The Greek Galen believed that blood was sucked from veins by the heart. William Harvey's careful experiments and work dissecting animals proved that the heart beats because it acts as a pump to circulate the blood around the body.

BLOOD ON THE MOVE

The Greek physician Galen believed food-laden blood was produced in the liver, and that it ebbed and flowed in the body, before being absorbed by the organs. Harvey took a fresh look at the heart's activity and came to a different conclusion. He cut up different animals and conducted experiments. He measured the amount of blood leaving the heart at a given time, and found that too much was passing through to be replaced; it was being recycled.

Arteries (colored red) carry oxygenated blood from heart to body

Heart pumps blood through pulmonary artery to lungs for oxygenation, and back via pulmonary vein

Both sides of heart act as pumps

Painting by Robert Hannah

THE KING'S PHYSICIAN

William Harvey was physician to England's King James I and his son, Charles I, whose support and interest helped him with his research. This 19th-century painting shows Harvey giving Charles I a demonstration of his theory of the circulation of blood. In one hand he holds a dissecting knife, in the other, he holds the heart of a deer killed in one of the king's royal parks.

CONTROVERSIAL BOOK

As a student at Padua University, in Italy, William Harvey was exposed to the latest ideas about anatomy. Hieronymous Fabricius (1537–1619), his teacher, identified valves in veins. Harvey later showed that these valves open to allow blood to flow toward the heart and then close to prevent it flowing back. This was a key to understanding the circulatory system. He gave lectures about his discoveries, but did not feel confident enough to venture into print until 1628. When his book was published, dedicated to the king, it caused a storm of controversy.

Drawings showing blood in veins flowing toward heart

Diagrams from William Harvey's book, *On the Motion of the Heart and Blood*

Veins (colored blue) return blood back to the heart

Small scissors

Scalpel

Medium scissors

"I began to think that there might be movement in a circle..."

WILLIAM HARVEY
in his book *On the Motion of the Heart and Blood*, published 1628

REPRODUCTION OF ANIMALS

Harvey was interested in reproduction, particularly in mammals. He had a theory that the females produced eggs that were fertilized by male sperm, and he put this to the test. With the permission of his patron, Charles I, he dissected the deer killed in weekly hunts in the royal parks. Although he failed to find an egg, his theory was proved to be correct over 200 years later.

Red deer

TOOLS FOR THE JOB

These instruments form part of a 17th-century surgical set. The instruments were carried around in a small case and would be used for delicate work in a physician's private practice. For dissection and surgery, William Harvey would have also required a set of tools of different sizes, some of them similar to those used in a butcher's shop or kitchen.

Robert Hooke

As CURATOR OF EXPERIMENTS at the Royal Society, Robert Hooke was at the center of intellectual life in late 17th-century London. He was part of a group interested in investigating the world of nature, but Hooke was exceptional. He was active in architecture, astronomy, chemistry, geology, mathematics, mechanics, medicine, meteorology, natural history, and optics. At weekly demonstrations to fellow Society members, he used scientific instruments he had built himself. After the Great Fire of 1666, he worked with Sir Christopher Wren (1632–1723) to rebuild the City of London. Despite his reputation and achievements, Hooke quarreled with Isaac Newton (pp. 22–23), and became increasingly reclusive. When he died, a huge sum of money was found in a chest in his house.

SIR ROBERT HOOKE (1635–1703)
No known portrait survives of the celebrated recluse, Robert Hooke. This painting was once thought to be of him. Writing in 1705, Richard Waller described Hooke as "an active, restless, indefatigable genius even almost to the last…"

BIRTH OF THE ROYAL SOCIETY
Statesman and philosopher Sir Francis Bacon (1561–1626) was a strong believer in experiment and investigation. Bacon inspired a group of people, including Hooke, who began to meet regularly in the 1640s to discuss his ideas. Among them were Robert Boyle and Christopher Wren, who went on to help found the Royal Society in 1660, now the world's leading institution for promoting scientific research.

BOYLE'S ASSISTANT
In 1655, Hooke was employed as an assistant by Irish-born aristocrat Robert Boyle (1627–91), author of a famous book on chemistry. Hooke helped Boyle to design and build an experiment in which an air pump (left) is used to create a vacuum. They observed how this affected things such as mice and candles placed inside the glass globe. Their research helped to prove Boyle's Law (1662), which defines what happens to a gas under pressure.

COMPOUND MICROSCOPE
Hooke made his observations through his compound microscope. A convex mirror with a lens was used to guide a light toward the subject, which was held in position by a pin. The body of the microscope was made of a series of tubes that moved up and down on a stand to focus. A lens at the lower end magnified the subject, and the eyepiece enlarged this image further.

> *"The most ingenious book I have ever read in my life."*
>
> **SAMUEL PEPYS**
> about *Micrographia* in his diary,
> January 21, 1665

Ant drawn under microscope

MICROGRAPHIA PAGE
A page from Hooke's book *Micrographia* unfolds, revealing an enormous picture of an ant shown in minute detail. He recorded his observations under a miscroscope, drawing tiny objects such as a flea, a bee sting, a snowflake, and an individual cell in a thin slice of cork. This book was one of the first published by the Royal Society and made Hooke world famous.

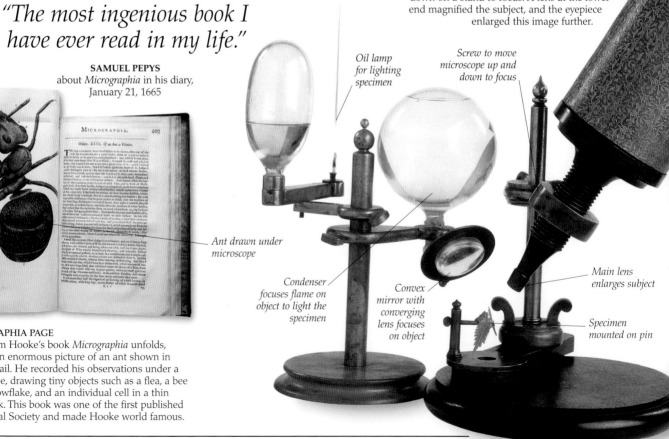

Oil lamp for lighting specimen

Screw to move microscope up and down to focus

Condenser focuses flame on object to light the specimen

Convex mirror with converging lens focuses on object

Main lens enlarges subject

Specimen mounted on pin

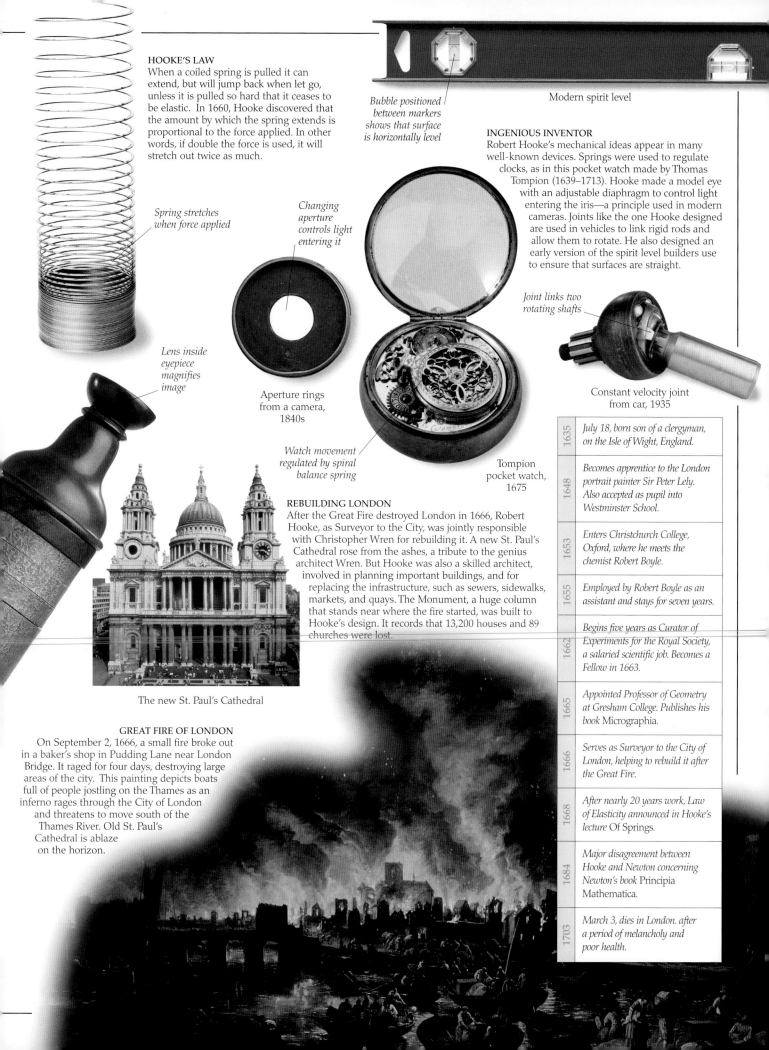

HOOKE'S LAW
When a coiled spring is pulled it can extend, but will jump back when let go, unless it is pulled so hard that it ceases to be elastic. In 1660, Hooke discovered that the amount by which the spring extends is proportional to the force applied. In other words, if double the force is used, it will stretch out twice as much.

Spring stretches when force applied

Bubble positioned between markers shows that surface is horizontally level

Modern spirit level

INGENIOUS INVENTOR
Robert Hooke's mechanical ideas appear in many well-known devices. Springs were used to regulate clocks, as in this pocket watch made by Thomas Tompion (1639–1713). Hooke made a model eye with an adjustable diaphragm to control light entering the iris—a principle used in modern cameras. Joints like the one Hooke designed are used in vehicles to link rigid rods and allow them to rotate. He also designed an early version of the spirit level builders use to ensure that surfaces are straight.

Changing aperture controls light entering it

Lens inside eyepiece magnifies image

Aperture rings from a camera, 1840s

Joint links two rotating shafts

Constant velocity joint from car, 1935

Watch movement regulated by spiral balance spring

Tompion pocket watch, 1675

REBUILDING LONDON
After the Great Fire destroyed London in 1666, Robert Hooke, as Surveyor to the City, was jointly responsible with Christopher Wren for rebuilding it. A new St. Paul's Cathedral rose from the ashes, a tribute to the genius architect Wren. But Hooke was also a skilled architect, involved in planning important buildings, and for replacing the infrastructure, such as sewers, sidewalks, markets, and quays. The Monument, a huge column that stands near where the fire started, was built to Hooke's design. It records that 13,200 houses and 89 churches were lost.

The new St. Paul's Cathedral

GREAT FIRE OF LONDON
On September 2, 1666, a small fire broke out in a baker's shop in Pudding Lane near London Bridge. It raged for four days, destroying large areas of the city. This painting depicts boats full of people jostling on the Thames as an inferno rages through the City of London and threatens to move south of the Thames River. Old St. Paul's Cathedral is ablaze on the horizon.

1635	*July 18, born son of a clergyman, on the Isle of Wight, England.*
1648	*Becomes apprentice to the London portrait painter Sir Peter Lely. Also accepted as pupil into Westminster School.*
1653	*Enters Christchurch College, Oxford, where he meets the chemist Robert Boyle.*
1655	*Employed by Robert Boyle as an assistant and stays for seven years.*
1662	*Begins five years as Curator of Experiments for the Royal Society, a salaried scientific job. Becomes a Fellow in 1663.*
1665	*Appointed Professor of Geometry at Gresham College. Publishes his book* Micrographia.
1666	*Serves as Surveyor to the City of London, helping to rebuild it after the Great Fire.*
1668	*After nearly 20 years work, Law of Elasticity announced in Hooke's lecture* Of Springs.
1684	*Major disagreement between Hooke and Newton concerning Newton's book* Principia Mathematica.
1703	*March 3, dies in London. after a period of melancholy and poor health.*

Isaac Newton

"I NOW DEMONSTRATE the frame of the System of the World," said Isaac Newton in his great book *Principia Mathematica*. This brilliant English mathematician and experimenter is one of the most important figures in the history of science. He set out a set of simple but fundamental laws using math to explain the forces that govern everything in the universe. Newton also explored the properties of light, and devoted himself to the mysterious art of alchemy. Although he preferred to work alone, he became involved in public life, first as a politician, then as Master of the Mint, responsible for England's coinage, and for 24 years as president of the Royal Society in London.

SIR ISAAC NEWTON (1642–1727)
Newton was a solitary, melancholy, and difficult man. He was highly competitive and had violent disagreements with other philosophers. In his research, he also took extraordinary risks, such as staring directly at the Sun and probing his own eye socket with a bodkin (small dagger).

FALLING APPLES
Legend has it that, as Newton sat in the garden of his home Woolsthorpe Manor, he watched an apple fall to the ground and pondered about the force that brought it down. He came up with the theory of universal gravitation, stating that the force that pulls two objects together (apple to the ground) depends on the mass of each object (how much matter it contains). The force dragging larger objects together is greater than that between smaller objects.

PLAGUE YEARS
In 1665, people fled the cities to escape the Great Plague, a disease that swept through England killing thousands. Cambridge University, where Newton was a student, had to close for a year. He retreated to his childhood home at Woolsthorpe Manor, Lincolnshire, where he developed the most revolutionary ideas about physics since those of Galileo (pp. 16–17).

Sun at center of solar system

Mercury

Venus

Orerry showing Earth's nearest planets

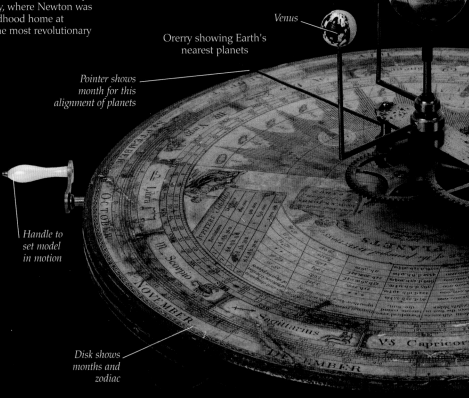

Pointer shows month for this alignment of planets

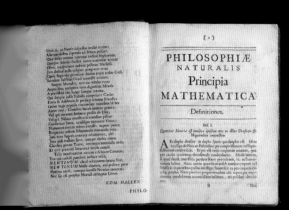

PHILOSOPHIÆ NATURALIS Principia MATHEMATICA Definitiones.

Handle to set model in motion

PRINCIPIA MATHEMATICA
The astronomer Edmond Halley (1656–1742) persuaded Newton to write down his ideas and offered to pay for their publication. The result was *Principia Mathematica* (published 1687), in which Newton set out three mathematical laws of motion to explain how forces (such as gravity) control the movement of objects. Newton's ideas greatly transformed people's understanding of the universe until the work of Einstein (pp. 46–47), and are still vitally important today.

Disk shows months and zodiac

First prism splits light into a spectrum of colors

Spectrum fans out

Narrow slit in screen lets only light of a single color pass through

Red light passes through slit

Red light meets second prism, which bends the light at an angle

Red light is unchanged by passing through prism

Some red light not bent because it "grazed," or did not pass through prism

SPLITTING LIGHT
While working at Woolsthorpe Manor, Newton projected a light beam through a slit in some shutters, watching it change into a rainbow of colors. He devised an experiment with two prisms to show that when white light is split into a band of colors, called the spectrum, they cannot be split further. This proved that the colors are a property of light, not the prisms. He describes his discoveries in his book *Opticks*.

Eyepiece lens

Light enters telescope here

Concave mirror inside bounces light up to eyepiece

Newton's reflecting telescope

REFLECTING TELESCOPE
The first telescopes were refracting telescopes. Light tends to break up into different colors as it passes through the lenses of these telescopes, giving images blurred colored edges. In 1668, Newton designed a new telescope that used mirrors to produce a sharper image. One mirror gathers light coming through the upper lens and reflects it on to a smaller mirror and on through another lens to the observer's eye. Reflectors are still used today in the Hubble Space Telescope and in huge telescopes in observatories. On the strength of this work, Newton was elected to the Royal Society, and he became its president in 1703.

> "If I have seen further, it is by standing on the shoulders of giants."

ISAAC NEWTON
writing to Hooke about Galileo and Kepler, 1676

Earth rotates as it revolves around the Sun

Moon circles Earth

PLANETARY MOTION
Turning the handle of this wind-up model, called an a orrery, sets the Earth and its nearest planets moving around the Sun. The German astronomer Johannes Kepler (1571–1630) explained planetary motion, but believed that it was caused by the Sun's magnetism. Newton calculated that every object in the universe attracts and is attracted by other objects. The force between the Sun and the planets is the same as the force that pulls an apple to the ground—gravity. This force holds the planets in place as they circle the Sun, and the Moon as it moves around the Earth.

THE ALCHEMIST
Newton spent 30 years working as an alchemist, exploring the nature of matter. In his laboratory in Cambridge, he did experiments and calculations, all carefully recorded in notebooks. Like many alchemists, he struggled to find the philosopher's stone—the magical substance that brings wisdom to its maker and changes base metals into gold—but he believed alchemy brought him closer to God.

1642	December 25, Newton born, a premature baby, at Woolsthorpe Manor, Lincolnshire, England.
1661	Enters Trinity College, Cambridge University.
1665	Returns to Woolsthorpe Manor, works on mathematics, optics, physics, astronomy, and calculus.
1668	Elected fellow of Trinity College, Cambridge.
1670	Lectures on optics at Cambridge.
1671	Demonstrates reflecting telescope to the Royal Society of London.
1672	Elected a fellow of the Royal Society, London.
1687	Principia Mathematica Book I is first published.
1696	Moves to London to become Warden of the Royal Mint.
1703	President of the Royal Society.
1704	Publishes Opticks.
1705	Knighted by Queen Anne.
1727	March 20, dies in Kensington, London. Body lies in state, then buried in Westminster Abbey.

Antoine-Laurent Lavoisier

LATE 18TH-CENTURY FRANCE was buzzing with new ideas in science and politics, and Antoine-Laurent Lavoisier was at the forefront of the changes they brought. A senior post at the Royal Gunpowder Administration in Paris provided him with a well-equipped laboratory, which became a powerhouse for experiments to refine the science we now know as chemistry. He identified 33 elements, gave oxygen its name, helped to explain the processes of combustion and respiration (breathing), reorganized scientific terms, and published the first modern chemistry textbook. Lavoisier was a supporter of social reform but, like many aristocrats, he was executed during the French Revolution's Reign of Terror.

ANTOINE-LAURENT LAVOISIER (1743–94)
Lavoisier had an excellent education that instilled a respect for reason as a means of understanding the natural world. He became a lawyer, but developed a passion for geology and chemistry.

1743	August 26, born in Paris, France, son of a wealthy family. Was a studious child.
1767	Works on the first geological map of France.
1768	Elected to the Academy of Sciences in France. Buys a share in a tax farm, giving him the right to collect certain taxes.
1771	Marries Marie Anne Pierrette Paulze, aged 13, daughter of the co-owner of his tax farm.
1774	English scientist Joseph Priestley discovers oxygen, but calls it phlogiston.
1775	Appointed Commissioner of the Royal Gunpowder Administration.
1778	Lavoisier recognizes and names oxygen.
1787	Publishes his book Method of Chemical Nomenclature, a system of names describing chemical compounds.
1788	Shows that air is a mixture of gases, which he calls oxygen and nitrogen.
1789	Publication of his Elementary Treatise of Chemistry, the first modern chemistry textbook. Mob storms the Bastille in Paris, marking the start of the French Revolution.
1794	May 8, dies. He is tried, found guilty, and beheaded on the same day, along with his father-in-law, by the French Revolutionary Government.

A WINNING TEAM
This ceramic relief portrays Lavoisier and his wife, Marie Anne, working together in the laboratory. She is shown recording data at a table, while he conducts an experiment. Her contribution to his work was invaluable. She learned English in order to translate the work of other scientists, hosted parties to discuss the latest ideas in chemistry, drew excellent illustrations of equipment and experiments for her husband's books, and wrote his memoirs.

CHEMICAL REVOLUTION
Balances were used in Lavoisier's laboratory to carry out weighing experiments to compare substances before and after chemical reactions such as burning. He demonstrated that a substance may change, but its weight remains the same. This led to the law of the conservation of mass, which states that although matter may change form, it cannot be created or destroyed. Lavoisier also classified elements, such as phosphorus, sulfur, carbon, and mercury, as substances that could not be decomposed into simpler ones (Mendeleyev, p. 40).

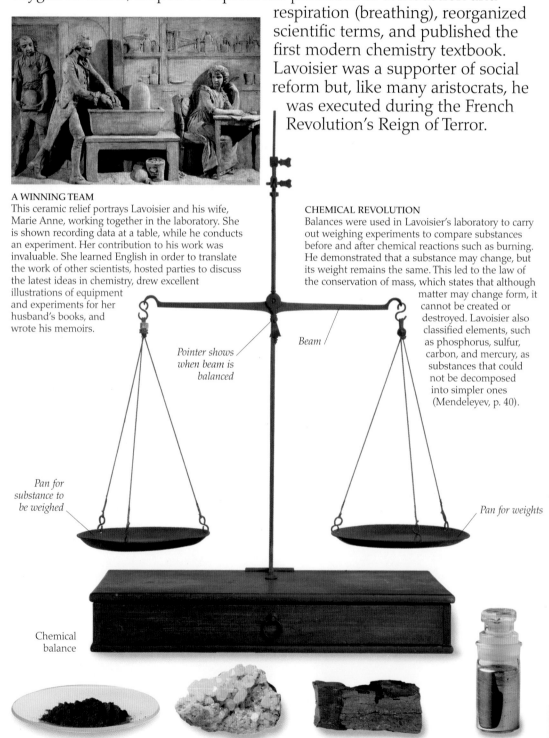

Pointer shows when beam is balanced

Beam

Pan for substance to be weighed

Pan for weights

Chemical balance

Red phosphorus

Sulfur

Carbon

Mercury

COMBUSTION

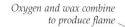

Oxygen and wax combine to produce flame

Wick carries fuel upward

As this candle burns, a chemical reaction called combustion is taking place. A fuel, in the form of vapor produced by the wax, combines with oxygen from air to produce heat and light, and form new compounds. One early theory suggested that part of the material being burned was released in the form of a colorless, weightless substance called phlogiston, though this was later found not to exist.

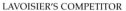

LAUGHING GAS

Demonstrations of pneumatic chemistry, as the study of gases was called at the time, were given at London's Royal Institution. This gave cartoonists a chance to poke fun at leading figures in science and politics. This German version of a cartoon by James Gillray shows a chemist with his apparatus giving laughing gas (nitrous oxide, which was discovered by Joseph Priestley), to the French emperor, Napoleon—with explosive results.

LAVOISIER'S COMPETITOR

Nonconformist English clergyman Joseph Priestley (1733–1804) was working on experiments with gases at the same time as Lavoiser. Priestley saw that carbon dioxide was produced by fermentation in a local brewery (which he called fixed air), and he invented carbonated water. He discovered 10 gases and showed by experiment that air was used up when animals breathe. He was the first to discover oxygen (1774), although he believed it was phlogiston.

Mercury in base of retort is heated forming calx (mercury oxide)

Retort linked to bell jar

Air in bell jar reduces as calx forms in retort

Heat source for experiment

NAMING OXYGEN

Lavoisier conducted a 12-day experiment to show that there are two parts to air, one of which combines with metals to form oxides and can support life. Mercury was heated in a special glass vessel called a retort, linked to a bell jar. A reddish substance called calx formed in the retort, and the volume of air reduced in the bell jar. The amount of air lost was equal to that released by the calx, when reheated. He called the released air oxygen.

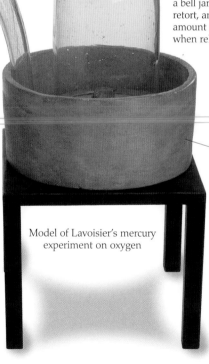

Trough contains more liquid mercury, which rises as air in the bell jar is reduced as air is released by calx

Model of Lavoisier's mercury experiment on oxygen

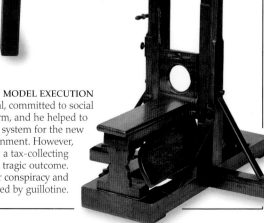

Scale model of a French guillotine

MODEL EXECUTION

Lavoisier was a liberal, committed to social and political reform, and he helped to establish the metric system for the new revolutionary government. However, his membership in a tax-collecting organization had a tragic outcome. He was arrested for conspiracy and beheaded by guillotine.

"It took them only an instant to cut off that head, and a hundred years may not produce another like it."

JOSEPH-LOUIS LAGRANGE,
a noted mathematician, on the execution of his colleague Lavoisier

Benjamin Franklin

1706	*January 17, born in Boston, Massachusetts, the tenth son of a soap and candle maker.*
1723	*Runs away to Philadelphia to become a printer's apprentice. Printing, writing, and publishing make him a wealthy man.*
1737	*Appointed postmaster of Philadelphia.*
1743	*Founds the American Philosophical Society to help scientific men discuss their discoveries. Also invents the heat-efficient Franklin stove.*
1746	*Begins extensive electrical experiments, using a Leyden jar, and begins a correspondence with Peter Collinson in London.*
1750	*Invents the lightning rod. To prove it would work, conducts electrical kite experiment two years later.*
1751	*Elected to the Pennsylvania Assembly. His electrical experiments are published.*
1753	*Receives Royal Society's Copley medal for work with electricity. Elected fellow three years later.*
1776	*Helps to draft and signs the American Declaration of Independence.*
1784	*Invents bifocal spectacles. Previous inventions include swimming fins.*
1790	*Dies on April 17. Buried in Philadelphia, Pennsylvania.*

IN THE 18TH CENTURY, little was known about the mysterious force now called electricity, until Benjamin Franklin began a series of experiments in his hometown of Philadelphia. In the most famous of these, he proved that lightning was a natural form of electrical charge. This extraordinary philosopher, inventor, and statesman began his career as a printer's apprentice and ended as a Founding Father of America's new democracy. He was at the forefront of revolutionary ideas in science and politics, and traveled frequently to Europe. His best-known inventions are the lightning conductor and bifocal spectacles, and he introduced words like negative, positive, and charge.

BENJAMIN FRANKLIN (1706–90)
This portrait of Franklin was painted in 1782, while he was in Paris as the United States' first ambassador to France. He also spent many years living in England, and was a popular member of society in both countries.

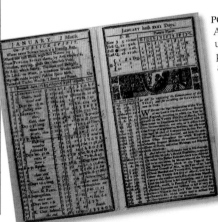

POOR RICHARD'S ALMANACK
An almanac is a collection of useful maxims, or proverbs. The pages of Franklin's classic almanac are peppered with sayings such as "haste makes waste." They reflect the humor and wide-ranging interests of the young printer who created *Poor Richard* in 1732. In the 20th edition, published in 1753, he included advice on "*How to secure Houses etc. from Lightning.*" Electricity became one of Franklin's most passionate interests.

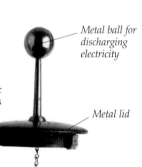

Metal ball for discharging electricity

Metal lid

Electrical charge flows down metal chain

Charge is stored in glass jar's metal coating

THE LEYDEN JAR
In 1745, a new device from the Netherlands made it possible to store electricity. Touching the ball and sides with a conducting material such as a forked metal rod creates a spark, releasing the charge built up inside the closed Leyden jar. Franklin started conducting his own experiments with the "miraculous bottle," in the company of friends in Philadelphia. Five letters to his friend Peter Collinson in London record his research in vivid detail.

THE ELECTRICAL KITE EXPERIMENT
To show how a lightning conductor works, Franklin made a silk kite with a pointed wire attached to the top, wrapped a dry silk scarf around his hand (to insulate his hand), and flew the kite in a thunderstorm. Attracted by the wire, lightning was drawn from the clouds down the wet string (a good conductor) to a metal key attached to a Leyden jar. If he held his knuckle close to the key it created a spark.

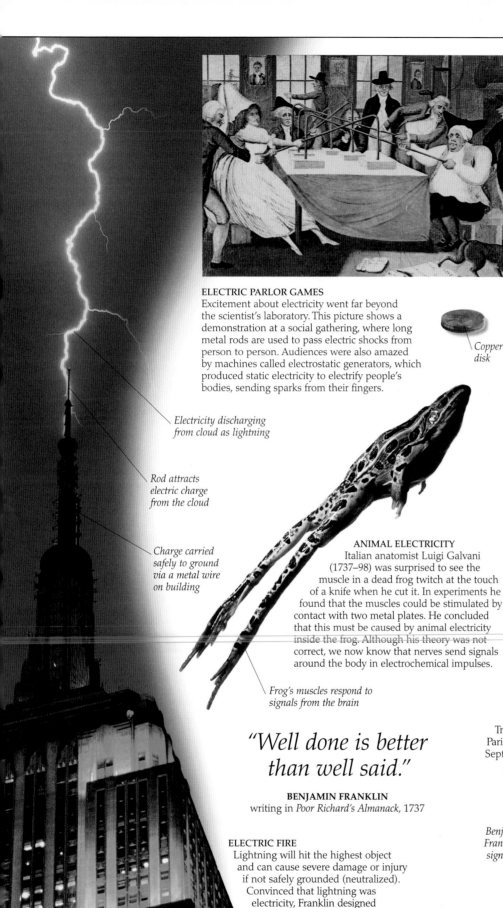

ELECTRIC PARLOR GAMES
Excitement about electricity went far beyond the scientist's laboratory. This picture shows a demonstration at a social gathering, where long metal rods are used to pass electric shocks from person to person. Audiences were also amazed by machines called electrostatic generators, which produced static electricity to electrify people's bodies, sending sparks from their fingers.

Glass rod supports disks

Zinc disk

Copper disk

Pasteboard disk

Voltaic pile

ELECTRIC CURRENT
Italian scientist Alessandro Volta (1745–1827) believed that metals produced electricity. He made an electric cell that combined two metals to create a flow of electricity. He used zinc and copper discs and between them pasteboard discs soaked in a solution of salt or acid, which reacts with the metals, producing a flow of electric charge. Piling up discs increased the flow of electric current that could be carried away along a wire. This was the first battery.

Electricity discharging from cloud as lightning

Rod attracts electric charge from the cloud

Charge carried safely to ground via a metal wire on building

ANIMAL ELECTRICITY
Italian anatomist Luigi Galvani (1737–98) was surprised to see the muscle in a dead frog twitch at the touch of a knife when he cut it. In experiments he found that the muscles could be stimulated by contact with two metal plates. He concluded that this must be caused by animal electricity inside the frog. Although his theory was not correct, we now know that nerves send signals around the body in electrochemical impulses.

Frog's muscles respond to signals from the brain

"Well done is better than well said."

BENJAMIN FRANKLIN
writing in *Poor Richard's Almanack*, 1737

Treaty of Paris, signed September 3, 1783

Benjamin Franklin's signature

ELECTRIC FIRE
Lightning will hit the highest object and can cause severe damage or injury if not safely grounded (neutralized). Convinced that lightning was electricity, Franklin designed a pointed lightning rod with a metal wire that runs all the way down a building, to draw the charge safely to the ground. Here lightning is drawn to a metal rod on top of New York's Empire State Building, which receives about 100 strikes every year.

SENIOR STATESMAN
Benjamin Franklin helped to negotiate for the Treaty of Paris, 1783, which confirmed the United States' independence from Britain. Franklin's intellect, personality, and scientific reputation made him a natural diplomat. London had become his second home, but he was committed to the Revolutionary War and returned home before war began in 1775. As one of the Founding Fathers of the US, his signature is also on the Declaration of Independence.

Joseph Banks

ENGLISH NATURALIST and explorer Joseph Banks traveled around the world on the first scientific voyage led by Captain James Cook (1728–79). By his return three years later, Banks had documented hundreds of previously unknown animals and plants. His lifelong enthusiasm for botany (study of plants) is reflected in every aspect of his career. He set up a herbarium of his collections in London and his house in Soho Square became a meeting place for the scientific community. As president of the Royal Society, London, his influence was far-reaching. Many of the specimens he collected are still studied by scientists today.

Bougainvillea, from Brazil

SIR JOSEPH BANKS (1743–1820)
This splendid portrait by Sir Joshua Reynolds shows Joseph Banks as a wealthy young man. By the age of 28, he had already acquired a considerable reputation as a botanist. The globe at his elbow is a tribute to his voyage with Captain Cook.

1743	February 13, Banks born in London, England, into a prosperous land-owning family.
1760	Begins studies at Oxford, where he develops a passion for botany. Receives a large family inheritance.
1766	Elected a fellow of the Royal Society. Travels to Newfoundland and Labrador aboard HMS Niger, to make plant, animal, and mineral collections.
1768	Leads the Royal Society delegation on a three-year global voyage with James Cook. Describes many new species on this voyage and brings back thousands of specimens.
1770	April 20, lands at Botany Bay on Australia's east coast. Later recommends that it should be colonized by convicts.
1772	Leads the first British scientific expedition to Iceland.
1778	Becomes president of the Royal Society—remaining for 42 years.
1781	Knighted for his services in scientific and public life.
1788	Becomes a founding member of London's Linnean Society, the world's oldest biological society.
1797	Becomes unofficial director of the Royal Botanic Gardens at Kew, working with George III to make it a center for botanical research.
1820	June 19, dies in Isleworth, Middlesex. Leaves his books and specimens to the British Museum.

CARL LINNAEUS
Swedish naturalist Carl Linnaeus (1707–78) is shown wearing a Lapland costume to celebrate his expedition there to find flora and fauna. He was an avid botanist and created a system for naming and classifying living things, based on their sexual characteristics. His method of naming plants is still used today. Linnaeus's pupil, Daniel Solander, accompanied Joseph Banks on his voyage with Captain Cook.

"No people went to sea better fitted out for the purpose of Natural History, nor more elegantly."

JOHN ELLIS
writing to Carl Linnaeus about Cook's first voyage, 1768

COOK'S FIRST VOYAGE
On August 12, 1768, a Royal Society expedition set sail from Plymouth on a scientific voyage to Tahiti, under the command of James Cook and with Banks aboard as botanist. The route took them from Madeira, off the west coast of Africa, across the Atlantic Ocean to South America, around Cape Horn to Tahiti in the South Pacific, then on to New Zealand, Australia, and South Africa, before returning to England. Banks's journal records details of the landscape, people, plants, and animals they saw on the way.

Kangaroo

Pressed specimen of Banksia serrata *collected on the voyage*

NAMING PLANTS
Banks carefully collected plants on the expedition and dried them between sheets of paper. On his return, the dried plants were stored in a collection called a herbarium. This *Banksia serrata* from Australia, painted by Sydney Parkinson, appears in Banks's book, the *Florilegium*, and was among many plants named after him. Using Linnaeus's system, it has been classified in the genus *Banksia*, and belongs to the species known as *serrata*—a Latin word that describes the serrated leaf edges.

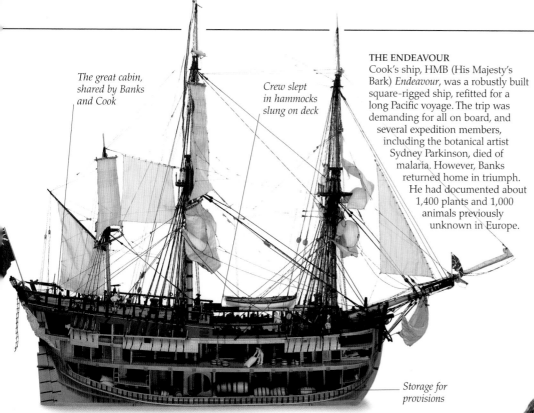

The great cabin, shared by Banks and Cook

Crew slept in hammocks slung on deck

Storage for provisions

Cross-section of the *Endeavour*

THE ENDEAVOUR

Cook's ship, HMB (His Majesty's Bark) *Endeavour*, was a robustly built square-rigged ship, refitted for a long Pacific voyage. The trip was demanding for all on board, and several expedition members, including the botanical artist Sydney Parkinson, died of malaria. However, Banks returned home in triumph. He had documented about 1,400 plants and 1,000 animals previously unknown in Europe.

POLYNESIAN PEOPLE

The *Endeavour* received a mixed reception from the people in the lands she visited. This painting is by Tupaia, a Polynesian high priest who Banks took on board the ship. It shows a Maori trader, resplendent in a feather cloak, offering Banks a piece of bark cloth in exchange for a crayfish. Other encounters were less successful. Skirmishes left several Maori people dead before the ship left New Zealand.

BREADFRUIT BOUNTY

Banks took a great interest in transplanting food plants across the globe. HMS *Bounty*, in the charge of Lieutenant William Bligh, was sent to transport breadfruit trees from Tahiti to Jamaica. Cast adrift by mutineers in 1789, Bligh traveled to safety with loyal members of his crew, and returned to Tahiti in 1791 to complete his mission.

Breadfruit

Banks's *Florilegium*

Illustration of Banksia serrata

Acacia tree (*Banksia sp.*)

Lattice lid allows light in

WARDIAN PLANT CASE

Plant collectors scoured the world for specimens for Joseph Banks, bringing them back to him at the Royal Botanical Gardens, Kew. With Banks as unofficial director, and with the support of George III, Kew became a world center for botanical research. The invention of the Wardian case in 1827 made the transport of living plants easier, since it provided a stable environment on long sea voyages. It was used at Kew until the 1960s.

Dried specimen of Hibiscus *from Banks's herbarium*

Georges Cuvier

WHEN **G**EORGES **C**UVIER **JOINED** the staff of the National Museum of Natural History in Paris in 1795, France was emerging from a turbulent political revolution. Cuvier used the museum's collections to forge an exceptional career studying animal anatomy. He was a brilliant lecturer and draftsman, and claimed he could reassemble a mammal skeleton from a single bone. As crates of specimens captured by French armies abroad flooded into the museum, he found evidence to support a theory that would shock his contemporaries. He observed that the fossil bones of prehistoric mammals, such as mammoths, are different from those of mammals alive today, and that these ancient beasts had completely died out. Cuvier was the founder of vertebrate paleontology (the study of fossils of extinct animals with backbones).

BARON GEORGES CUVIER
(1769–1832)
This portrait by Marie-Nicholas Ponce-Camus, who also painted Napoleon, shows Cuvier looking every inch the gentleman. From quite modest origins, he became a member of the French academic elite and survived many political upheavals.

1769	*August 23, born in Montbéliard, in the Jura region of France.*
1784	*Begins four years of study at the Carolinian Academy in Stuttgart, then tutors a French family in the early years of the Revolution.*
1795	*Joins the National Museum of Natural History, Paris.*
1799	*Becomes Professor of Natural History at the Collège de France.*
1801	*Begins research on fish, leading to* The Natural History of Fish.
1802	*Begins work on mollusks (animals such as slugs, snails, and squid).*
1804	*Observes that age of fossil mammals found around Paris suggests that the Earth was much older than accepted at that time.*
1808	*Placed on the council of the Imperial University by Napoleon.*
1812	*Publishes* Researches on Fossil Bones, *reporting 29 new species.*
1813	*Publishes his* Essay on the Theory of the Earth.
1817	*Publishes* The Animal Kingdom, *with his own illustrations.*
1826	*Made a Grand Officer of the Legion of Honor and in 1831 becomes a baron and is appointed president of the Council of State.*
1832	*Nominated to the Ministry of the Interior. Dies of cholera, May 13.*

Imprint of brachiopod fossil (shelled marine animal)

Shelly rock from the top of Mount Snowdon, Wales

MYSTERIOUS ROCK SHELLS
Shells preserved in stone can be found high up on mountaintops. Many 18th-century Europeans believed they were left by the Biblical flood. However, naturalists were finding evidence that the Earth's surface had gradually changed. The shells were fossils, the remains of animals that fell into soft sediment at the bottom of ancient oceans. This sediment hardened into rock that was later forced upward to form mountains.

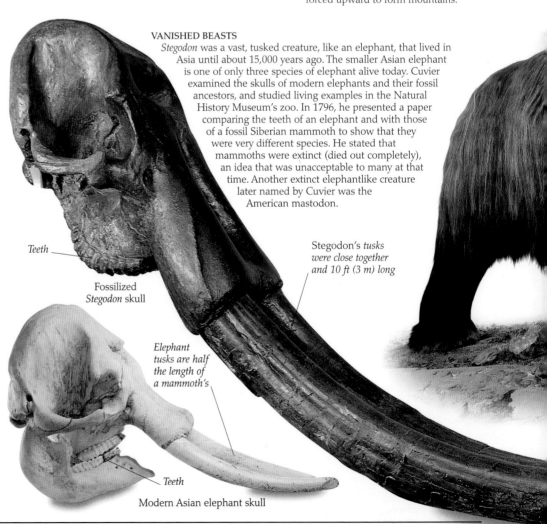

VANISHED BEASTS
Stegodon was a vast, tusked creature, like an elephant, that lived in Asia until about 15,000 years ago. The smaller Asian elephant is one of only three species of elephant alive today. Cuvier examined the skulls of modern elephants and their fossil ancestors, and studied living examples in the Natural History Museum's zoo. In 1796, he presented a paper comparing the teeth of an elephant and with those of a fossil Siberian mammoth to show that they were very different species. He stated that mammoths were extinct (died out completely), an idea that was unacceptable to many at that time. Another extinct elephantlike creature later named by Cuvier was the American mastodon.

Teeth

Fossilized *Stegodon* skull

Stegodon's *tusks were close together and 10 ft (3 m) long*

Elephant tusks are half the length of a mammoth's

Teeth

Modern Asian elephant skull

FOSSIL FINDS

These fossil-hunters are digging out bones at a prehistoric site in Durfort in the south of France. They belong to the huge *Mammuthus meridionalis*, or southern mammoth, that roamed across Europe and died out about a million years ago. During the 18th and 19th centuries, an increase in quarrying and road, rail, and canal construction uncovered large fossils.

CHANGING FORMS

Cuvier's colleague, French naturalist Jean Baptiste de Lamarck (1774–1829), was an expert on invertebrates (animals without backbones), who proposed an early theory of evolution. Cuvier was convinced that animals' characteristics were fixed and did not change. Lamarck proposed that living things evolve, adapting their forms to suit different circumstances. These four butterflies found in parts of South America belong to different subspecies (groups within a species). They can interbreed, but are slightly different from each other in appearance. Lamarck was right about living things evolving but not in his method.

Agrias claudina lugens,
Peru

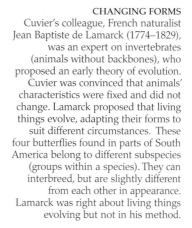

Agrias claudina godmani,
central Brazil

Agrias claudina claudianus,
southeastern Brazil

Agrias claudina intermedius,
southeastern Columbia, Venezuela

> *"Life on this earth has often been disturbed by dreadful events."*

GEORGES CUVIER
in his book *Revolutionary Upheavals on the Surface of the Globe*, 1825

Woolly mammoth

Skull structure very different from elephants alive today

Fossilized mastodon vertebra

VANISHED WORLDS AND SPECIES

Supervolcanoes, earthquakes, and massive floods can have a devastating effect on living things. Cuvier was convinced that due to a series of catastrophic events in Earth's history, some species of animals had become extinct, and surviving species had moved in to take their place. His theory was published in *Essay on the Theory of the Earth*. He was the first person to provide evidence for extinctions, now known to be an important part of the history of life.

Charles Darwin

As a young student, Charles Darwin seemed destined for a career in medicine or the Church, but natural history was his passion. When in 1831 he was offered the opportunity to become the naturalist on the research ship HMS *Beagle,* he accepted at once. The voyage introduced him to the varied wildlife and geology of half the globe and sowed the seeds of an idea that would later transform the understanding of the history of life. He began to develop the theory that all species derive from previously existing species, and that this process, called evolution, is due to natural selection. For many years Darwin gathered scientific evidence, but he remained silent until naturalist Alfred Wallace (1823–1913) expressed similar ideas in 1858. Darwin's *On the Origin of Species* was published in 1859.

CHARLES DARWIN (1809–82)
Darwin grew his trademark white beard in later life. As a young man he was tall, with brown hair, and healthy enough to embark on a long voyage. On his return, he suffered for 40 years with symptoms that may have been caused by a parasitic disease picked up on his travels.

1809	*February 12, Darwin born in Shropshire, England. His grandfathers were the physician and philosopher Erasmus Darwin and the potter Josiah Wedgwood.*
1825	*Enters Edinburgh University, Scotland to study medicine but loses interest.*
1827	*Enrolls in Christ's College, Cambridge University for a BA. Starts a collection of beetles. Visits the Royal Institution, Linnaean Society, and Zoological Gardens in London.*
1831	*Accompanies Adam Sedgwick (1785–1873) Professor of Geology at Cambridge on a field trip to North Wales. Begins a five-year voyage on board HMS Beagle.*
1837	*Gives his first speech to the Geological Society in London.*
1838	*Publishes volume one of Zoology, one of five books on fossil mammals. collected on Beagle voyage.*
1839	*Elected fellow of the Royal Society. The Voyage of the Beagle—a memoir of his journey—published as Journal and Remarks.*
1859	*Publishes On the Origin of Species by Means of Natural Selection, provoking controversy.*
1871	*Publishes The Descent of Man, expanding his evolutionary ideas.*
1882	*April 19, dies of a heart attack. He is buried in Westminster Abbey.*

VOYAGE OF THE BEAGLE
"Tell Edward to send me up my carpet bag," wrote Darwin to his sister, "my slippers, a pair of lightish walking shoes, my Spanish books, my new microscope, … my geological compass." Darwin was joining the HMS *Beagle* on a five-year voyage (1831–36). The ship went to the Cape Verde Islands, in the Atlantic, along the South American coast, across the Pacific to Australia, and to Mauritius, off the coast of East Africa. Darwin returned with a diary and a huge collection of specimens.

Part of Darwin's beetle collection

Darwin's signature

Compass

Telescope used on *Beagle*

Butterfly wing

Collecting boxes from Down House with Darwin's specimens

Vermillion flycatcher

GIANT TORTOISE
HMS *Beagle* visited the Galapagos, rugged volcanic islands in the Pacific, 800 miles (1,300 km) off Ecuador, South America. Darwin was puzzled by the unique wildlife he found there. Locals pointed out that the giant tortoises on each island were slightly different. Darwin also noticed that the shapes of the beaks of the island finches varied according to the food they ate. He later concluded that one species had arrived from the mainland and, from this, new island species had developed.

Giant tortoise

Model of *Glyptodon*

Armadillo-like scales

Modern armadillo

EVIDENCE FOR CHANGE

On his voyage on the *Beagle*, Darwin read *The Principles of Geology* by Charles Lyell (1797–1875), and saw for himself evidence of how Earth's landscapes had been shaped over hundreds of millions of years. He also collected fossils of extinct animals in South America, and noticed the similarities between the vast armored extinct *Glyptodon* and the smaller living armadillo. Unlike Lyell, who believed that species could not change, Darwin thought that the *Glyptodon* must be the armadillo's ancestor.

First sketch of a species family tree

Page from Darwin's *Tree of Life* notebook, 1837

THEORY OF NATURAL SELECTION

Darwin's sketches links different living organisms in family trees showing that animals and plants are related. He shows that evolution happens through natural selection. This means that some individuals in a species survive better than others, because they have features, such as sharper claws, that suit their environment. They then pass on this advantage to their offspring, a process that continues with future generations.

> *"I have called this principle, by which each slight variation, if useful, is preserved, by the term Natural Selection."*

CHARLES DARWIN
On the Origin of Species, 1859

CONTROVERSY

"It's like confessing to a murder," wrote Darwin about his revolutionary book, *On the Origin of Species*. By tracing living things back to a common ancestor, he showed that humans were related to animals. This challenged the Christian view of creation. Darwin had delayed publishing his theory because he expected a hostile reaction. This came from the Church and many scientists. Cartoons like this, depicting him as an ape, illustrate how his ideas were mocked in the press.

Cartoon in *Hornet* magazine, 1871

Darwin's pen

Microscope slide

Darwin's *Beagle* notebook

DOWN HOUSE

In 1842 Darwin moved to Down House, Kent. Here he lived quietly, working on evolution, earthworms, and orchids. Ever the naturalist, he even noted down his young children's developing facial expressions for a book he was writing on human emotions. He was a loving parent and was distraught when one of his daughters, Annie, died at the age of 10. Down house is now preserved as a museum.

CHARLES BABBAGE (1791–1871)
His main interests were mathematics (he had a passion for statistics), manufacturing, technology, and political economy. Babbage also helped found several learned societies. He was a quirky character, a popular dinner guest, who could be temperamental and difficult at times.

1791	December 26, born in London, England. Brought up and married Georgiana Whitmore, in Devon.
1810	Accepted into Trinity College, Cambridge, but disappointed by the level of mathematical instruction available.
1812	Sets up the Analytical Society with fellow undergraduates John Herschel and George Peacock.
1814	Graduates with a BA from Peterhouse College, Cambridge.
1816	Elected fellow of the Royal Society, London.
1819	Begins to construct a small Difference Engine, a calculating machine that is completed by 1822.
1820	Elected a fellow of The Royal Society of Edinburgh. Helps found the Royal Astronomical Society.
1823	Receives a gold medal from the Royal Astronomical Society for the development of his Difference Engine. Starts working on a second, larger, machine.
1827	Becomes Lucasian Professor of Mathematics at Cambridge University. Remains for 12 years, but never lectures.
1833	Meets Ada Lovelace, who translates an Italian paper on his Analytical Engine for him.
1836	Plans for the Analytical Engine completed, but it was never built.
1871	Dies October 18 in London, in relative obscurity.

Charles Babbage

Throughout his life, Charles Babbage worked on designs for huge automated calculating machines. He was a gifted mathematician from a wealthy background with a variety of practical and scientific interests. Saturday evening parties parties at his London home were filled with educated society guests. He had a particular passion for printed astronomical and mathematical tables, which drove him to design his great machines; he wanted to make the tables free from human errors. Babbage spent a fortune on his ambitious projects, but died a disappointed man—although he is now hailed as a pioneer of modern computing. In 1991, a full-scale working model of his Difference Engine No 2 was completed by London's Science Museum. Its printer, with over 4,000 parts and weighing over three tonnes, was finished nine years later.

Windows show answers to calculation

Wheels represent numbers 0–9

The Pascaline manual calculator

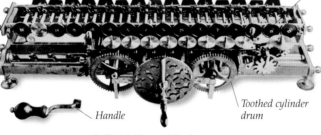

Handle

Toothed cylinder drum

Leibniz's Stepped Reckoner

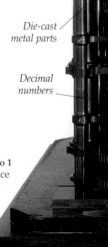

Rows of toothed wheels rotated by stepped drum inside machine

Die-cast metal parts

Decimal numbers

MANUAL CALCULATORS
French philosopher Blaise Pascal (1623–62) and German mathematician Gottfried von Leibniz (1646–1716) both designed mechanical calculators. In the Pascaline calculator, figures were calculated by turning a series of toothed wheels that brought up the answers in corresponding windows. Leibniz refined this design in the Stepped Reckoner, made in 1694, which could add, subtract, and do multiplication and division more efficiently.

BABBAGE'S DIFFERENCE ENGINE No 1
In 1821 Babbage started work on his first large-scale Difference Engine, a machine designed to carry out auomatic calculations. The impressive piece of equipment would have required 25,000 die-cast metal parts and weighed 15 tons. This small section, made by toolmaker Joseph Clement, was finished in 1832. It is also the oldest surviving example of an automatic calculator. The rest of the Engine was never built. Babbage received government funding for the project, but after many setbacks it was abandoned, so he started on Difference Engine No. 2.

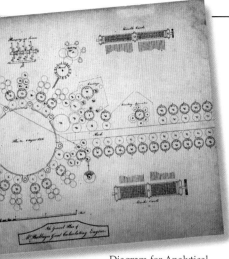
Diagram for Analytical
Engine, 1840

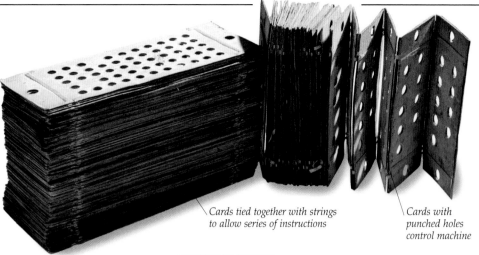
Punched cards for
Analytical Engine

Cards tied together with strings
to allow series of instructions

Cards with
punched holes
control machine

ANALYTICAL ENGINE

In 1833 Babbage moved on from his Difference Engines to the Analytical Engine—a more sophisticated machine that could be programmed for a specific purpose, using strings of cards punched with holes. Like the modern computer, it was to hold figures in a memory called a store, and have a central processing unit called a mill. The Analytical Engine required even more parts than the Difference Engine, and a steam engine to drive it, so was never built.

Toothed wheel

"The Analytical Engine weaves algebraical patterns just as the Jacquard-loom weaves flowers and leaves."

ADA LOVELACE
in her notes on the translation of Menebrae's paper on the
Analytical Engine, published 1842

ADA LOVELACE

A gifted society hostess, Lady Lovelace (1815–52), daughter of Lord Byron, became a great supporter of Babbage's Analytical Engine. She suggested a method for using it to calculate Bernoulli numbers, now recognized as an early computer program. Ada Lovelace and Babbage exchanged lively letters about music and horse racing as well as mathematics.

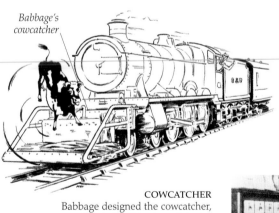
Babbage's
cowcatcher

COWCATCHER

Babbage designed the cowcatcher, or pilot, in 1838 to clear obstacles such as stray animals, from railroad tracks. This was a metal frame that projected from the front of a train engine to push the obstruction out of its path. He conducted other safety experiments for the Great Western Railway. An avid supporter of industrial progress, he drew on his mechanical experience in his influential book, *On the Economy of Machinery and Manufactures*, published in 1832.

HOLLERITH'S PUNCHED CARDS

In 1801, French weaver Joseph-Marie Jacquard invented a system of punched cards to control patterns on his looms. Statistician Herman Hollerith (1860–1929) used the idea to program his tabulating machine, seen in this photograph, to process data from the 1890 American census.

Michael Faraday

SIR MICHAEL FARADAY (1791–1867)
Together with his wife, Sarah, Michael Faraday was a member of a Christian sect, founded in Scotland, called the Sandemanians. His beliefs led him to look for unified laws in nature, but he kept his life as a natural philosopher completely separate from his life as a pastor.

As a poor apprentice bookbinder in London, Michael Faraday had little education, but in 1812 a free ticket to lectures by leading chemist Sir Humphry Davy (1778–1829) transformed his life. Employed by Davy as a chemical assistant, he accompanied him on a scientific tour of Europe. By 1821, Faraday became superintendent of the well-equipped laboratory at London's Royal Institution. He was a dedicated experimental scientist, and became fascinated by electromagnetism (magnetism caused by a moving electric charge). Faraday devised a method of using a magnetic field to produce a continuous electric current, and applied this in a design for an early version of the electric motor and a dynamo, a device that converts mechanical movement into electric power.

1791	September 22, Faraday born in London, son of a blacksmith from the north of England.
1805	Apprenticed as a bookbinder to George Riebau.
1810	Joins the City Philosophical Society, a group that meets weekly to discuss and hear lectures on scientific topics.
1813	Appointed as Davy's chemical assistant at the Royal Institution.
1821	Promoted to Superintendent of the Royal Institution.
1830	Becomes Professor of Chemistry at the Royal Military Academy in Woolwich; remains there 21 years.
1831	Discovers electromagnetic induction, the principle behind the electric transformer and generator.
1836	Appointed scientific adviser to Trinity House, the lighthouse authority for England in charge of safe navigation in the coastal waters of England and Wales.
1845	Discovers diamagnetism—that magnetism is exhibited in a substance in the presence of a magnetic field. Also establishes that magnetic force and light are related.
1867	August 25, dies in London.

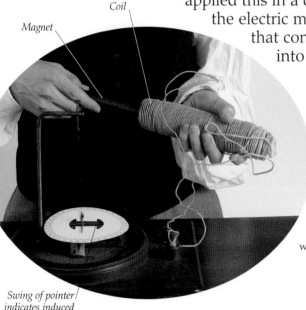

Magnet

Coil

Swing of pointer indicates induced current

MAGNETIC FIELD
One of Faraday's most famous experiments proved that a magnetic field could produce an electric current—a process called induction. In 1831, he demonstrated that moving a magnet in and out of a wire coil produces a force that registers on a galvanometer (a machine that detects and measures electric current). He believed that "lines of force" surround an electrically charged object, similar to patterns that appear when iron filings are sprinkled around a magnet.

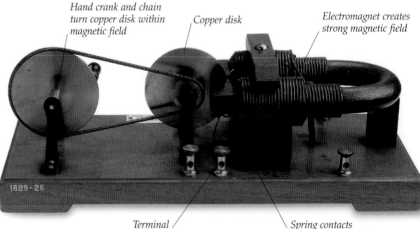

Hand crank and chain turn copper disk within magnetic field

Copper disk

Electromagnet creates strong magnetic field

Terminal

Spring contacts

CHILDREN'S CHRISTMAS LECTURES
A rapt audience of children watch Faraday at one of his annual Christmas Day lectures, later published in a classic book, *The History of a Candle*. He was an exceptional communicator, committed to taking science to a wider audience. The Christmas lectures by leading scientists for young people continue in the Royal Institution to this day.

ELECTRIC MOTOR
In 1831 Faraday devoted his time to investigating electromagnetism, and made the first example of an electric generator. In this model, a copper disk spins between the poles of an electromagnet, producing electromotive force. If terminals on the base link the copper disk in the circuit to a galvanometer, the galvanometer will indicate a steady flow of current. When the disk stops, the current ceases.

Thomas Edison

The "Wizard of Menlo Park," Thomas Edison, was a tireless inventor and shrewd businessman. His inventing career began when he was a young telegraph operator, and he went on to establish a highly productive laboratory in Menlo Park, New Jersey. He researched 3,000 different materials for filaments in the search for a long-lasting electric lightbulb. He set up an electrical distribution company—a pioneering step in the mass production of electricity—and exploited the potential of this energy source to transform work, home, and entertainment.

THOMAS ALVA EDISON 1847–1931
Edison displays the kinetoscope, a peephole viewer and forerunner to the projector, designed by his assistant William Dickson. This coincided with the birth of the motion picture industry in a studio called the Black Maria, at Edison's West Orange Laboratory, New Jersey.

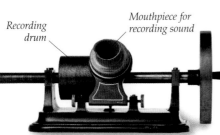

Recording drum

Mouthpiece for recording sound

Edison's phonograph

Carbon filament glows when heated

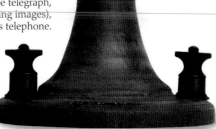

Vacuum in bulb prevents filament from burning up

Electric current heats carbon filament

Edison's incandescent lightbulb

"Genius is one percent inspiration, 99 percent perspiration."

THOMAS EDISON
Harper's Monthly magazine, published September 1932

THE WIZARD INVENTOR
Edison was notoriously hardworking—he even returned to his laboratory on his wedding day. He improved on the ideas of others to produce the first commercial incandescent lightbulb. Teams of people were employed in his laboratories and he patented over 1,000 inventions. Among those actually produced were the electrical vote recorder, the phonograph (for recording and replaying sound), the ticker-tape telegraph, the kinetograph (an early camera to create moving images), and an improved design for Bell's telephone.

FRED OTT'S SNEEZE
This motion picture was made in 1889 in Edison's New Jersey studio. Every stage of a sneeze by laboratory worker Fred Ott is recorded in a series of images on film. A viewing machine called a kinetoscope passed the images through a viewer. Edison was inspired by the work of Eadweard Muybridge (1830–1904), who used hundreds of frames to capture movement.

THE AGE OF ELECTRICITY
New York City's streets are illuminated by a blaze of neon lights. In 1882 Edison helped to build the Pearl Street power plant for the south of Manhattan. He was determined to break the monopoly of gas, which was the main power source for street lights. As electricity became supplied on a grid system, a huge market developed for the electrical components Edison manufactured.

1847	*February 11, born in Ohio; is homeschooled by his mother.*
1862	*Starts work as a telegraph operator in Port Huron, Michigan.*
1868	*Invents the electric vote recorder, his first patented invention.*
1876	*Moves to Menlo Park, New Jersey, and establishes his first full-scale industrial research laboratory.*
1877	*Invents the carbon microphone, used in telephone handsets to transmit sound.*
1879	*Gives first demonstration of the incandescent lightbulb.*
1881	*Forms the Edison Electric Light Company in New York City.*
1893	*Demonstrates and patents his system for making and showing motion pictures.*
1909	*Markets the Alkaline storage battery, now used in numerous commercial applications.*
1931	*October 18, dies at home in West Orange, New Jersey, now maintained as the Edison National Historic Site.*

Louis Pasteur

THE ROLE OF BACTERIA, and other microscopic organisms (so small they can only be seen under a microscope) in causing disease was a mystery in the early 19th century. Many people believed that infections could appear spontaneously, out of the air or in living matter. The French biochemist Louis Pasteur was the first person to prove that microbes reproduce. His germ theory of disease revolutionized medical science, and he urged hospitals to use hygiene practices, such as handwashing, to prevent the spread of infection. Through patient, methodical work and careful experimentation, Pasteur tracked down dangerous microorganisms, and went on to develop vaccines to protect both animals and humans from some of the most feared diseases.

LOUIS PASTEUR (1822–95)
Finnish artist Albert Edelfelt spent weeks in Louis Pasteur's laboratory making sketches for this portrait in the 1880s. Pasteur was already a world-famous scientist and is shown examining a piece of spinal column for his research on rabies.

LIFE FROM LIFE
The tiny natural yeasts covering these grapes are single-celled fungi that grow by budding off parts of their cells. People used to believe that microorganisms like these appeared as if from nowhere, springing into life where conditions were suitable— a theory known as spontaneous generation. Pasteur used his experiments to prove that microscopic organisms are actually produced by living things like themselves.

Colored water prevents air entering

Carbon dioxide bubbles out through water

Bung to keep out microorganisms

Yeast-covered grapes

Sugar works with yeast to produce alcohol

Budding yeast cell

> *"In the field of observation, chance favors the prepared mind."*
>
> **LOUIS PASTEUR**
> from his inaugural lecture at the University of Lille, 1854

Carbon dioxide gas bubbles form as yeast converts sugar to alcohol

HEALTHY MILK
Before milk goes on sale, it has to be heated gently to a specific temperature for a specified period of time to reduce the number of harmful organisms (such as bacteria, viruses, and molds) that it may contain. This technique is called pasteurization, after Pasteur, who first used it in the mid 1860s to improve fermenting wine.

Grape juice and sugar fermenting

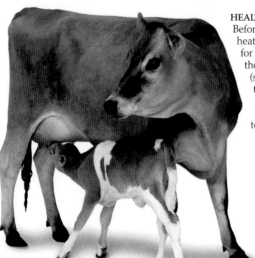

IMPROVING FERMENTATION OF ALCOHOL
The French wine and beer industry asked for Pasteur's help because they often had to throw away sour batches of their products. Pasteur detected differences in shape between yeast cells in good and sour wine. He discovered that living yeast produced alcohol (1856), even though the fermentation process was oxygen free. The correct yeast had to be used, and other microorganisms removed by heating the liquid to 122°F (55°C).

SAVING THE SILKWORM

Southwest France had a flourishing silkworm industry that supplied silk for Paris fashions. In 1864, the government asked Pasteur to help the silkworm breeders, whose cocoons were ravaged by disease. Locals were skeptical about the scientist with a microscope; but he proved to be their saviour. After two years Pasteur found that the infection was caused by two types of parasite. All infected worms, eggs, and the mulberry leaves they fed on, were destroyed.

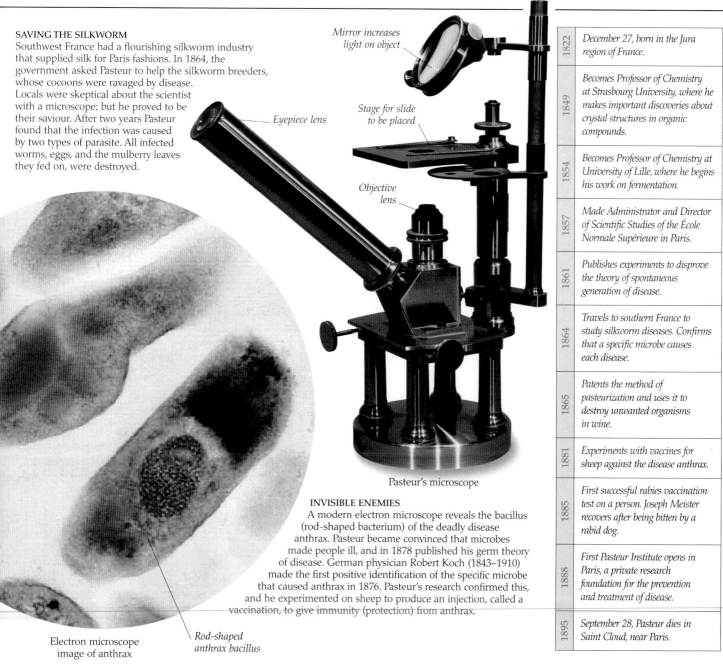

Mirror increases light on object

Eyepiece lens

Stage for slide to be placed

Objective lens

Pasteur's microscope

Electron microscope image of anthrax

Rod-shaped anthrax bacillus

INVISIBLE ENEMIES

A modern electron microscope reveals the bacillus (rod-shaped bacterium) of the deadly disease anthrax. Pasteur became convinced that microbes made people ill, and in 1878 published his germ theory of disease. German physician Robert Koch (1843–1910) made the first positive identification of the specific microbe that caused anthrax in 1876. Pasteur's research confirmed this, and he experimented on sheep to produce an injection, called a vaccination, to give immunity (protection) from anthrax.

1822	December 27, born in the Jura region of France.
1849	Becomes Professor of Chemistry at Strasbourg University, where he makes important discoveries about crystal structures in organic compounds.
1854	Becomes Professor of Chemistry at University of Lille, where he begins his work on fermentation.
1857	Made Administrator and Director of Scientific Studies of the École Normale Supérieure in Paris.
1861	Publishes experiments to disprove the theory of spontaneous generation of disease.
1864	Travels to southern France to study silkworm diseases. Confirms that a specific microbe causes each disease.
1865	Patents the method of pasteurization and uses it to destroy unwanted organisms in wine.
1881	Experiments with vaccines for sheep against the disease anthrax.
1885	First successful rabies vaccination test on a person. Joseph Meister recovers after being bitten by a rabid dog.
1888	First Pasteur Institute opens in Paris, a private research foundation for the prevention and treatment of disease.
1895	September 28, Pasteur dies in Saint Cloud, near Paris.

RABID DOG

Saliva foams at the mouth of this dog, indicating that it is suffering from rabies. The disease is caused by a virus—a tiny organism too small to be detected by Pasteur's microscope. He realized that the disease affects the central nervous system and, by extracting fluid from the spinal columns of infected animals, he produced a vaccine that worked successfully on dogs.

FIRST RABIES VACCINE

In 1885, nine-year-old Joseph Meister was the first person to receive a vaccination to prevent the onset of rabies, a terrible disease transmitted by a bite from an infected dog. Pasteur had discovered that a weaker strain of the disease could give animals immunity to it, but he had been reluctant to test the vaccine on a human. He was very relieved when the boy made a successful recovery.

Rabies virus causes dog to foam at the mouth

1834	*February 8, Mendeleyev born in Tobolsk, Siberia, Russia.*
1849	*Travels to Moscow to apply to college, but is not accepted.*
1850	*Enrols as a student teacher at St. Petersburg Pedagogical Institute.*
1859	*Studies under Robert Bunsen (1811–1899) in Germany.*
1864	*Becomes professor at Technological Institute, St. Petersburg.*
1867	*Appointed Professor of Chemistry at St. Petersburg University and starts famous textbook in 1868.*
1869	*Produces the first effective version of the Periodic Table of the Elements.*
1876	*Sent by government to US to study production of petroleum.*
1882	*Receives Davy Medal jointly with German chemist Lothar Meyer (1830–95).*
1890	*Resigns professorship in support of protesting students.*
1893	*Appointed director of the Bureau of Weights and Measures.*
1907	*February 2, dies of influenza in St. Petersburg.*

Dmitry Mendeleyev

WHEN RUSSIAN CHEMISTRY PROFESSOR Dmitry Mendeleyev first began to plan a textbook for his students in 1869, there were 63 known elements—now 117 have been identified. These were not the elements of Aristotle (pp. 7–8), but the single substances that form the basis of all matter, which are often bound together into materials called compounds. In the 19th century, chemists developed new techniques that allowed them to split up compounds and isolate more elements. As knowledge grew about atoms (the units that make up elements), scientists began to look at ways of classifying elements. Mendeleyev arranged them in a Periodic Table that has become the cornerstone of modern chemistry.

WHAT IS AN ELEMENT?
An element is a substance made up of only one type of atom, which cannot be broken down into other substances. Embedded in this rock is gold, a metallic element. Elements can occur naturally, like gold, or can be isolated artificially, like phosphorus, from compounds (substances made from a combination of two or more elements).

Gold embedded in quartz rock

Sodium

ORDERING THE ELEMENTS
When Mendeleyev devised his Periodic Law and table, he was among several chemists trying to put elements into some kind of order. One approach was to sort them by physical properties, such as hardness, color, and brittleness, much as you might describe people by appearance. Another approach was to sort them by their chemical properties—for example, how they react with other substances, or at what temperature they melt. Copper (Cu), for example, is a reddish metal, softer than iron, and easy to bend. Magnesium (Mg) catches fire when heated. Silvery mercury (Hg) is the only metal that is liquid at room temperature.

Bromine

Iron

Zinc

Copper

ST. PETERSBURG'S PROFESSOR
In the Russian city of St. Petersburg, the apartment where Mendeleyev lived while he was a professor at the university is preserved as a museum. He was immensely popular with his students, and used his own success to raise the profile of scientists in Russia. The lack of a good chemistry textbook for students prompted him to write one of his own—*Principles of Chemistry*.

ISOLATION OF PURE POTASSIUM
The English chemist Sir Humphry Davy (1778–1829) was famous for inventing a miners' safety lamp, but he also discovered new elements. Using an electric current, he melted potash and soda (now called potassium carbonate and sodium carbonate) to produce small shiny globules. This isolated two metallic elements, potassium and sodium, by a process that was later called electrolysis. Davy's brother described him dancing with joy at his success.

Battery provides electric current

Wire carries electric current

Potash melted by electric current

ATOMIC WEIGHT
In 1808 English scientist John Dalton (1776–1844) proposed that each element is made up of atoms of the same size and that the atoms of different elements could be identified by their weight. Atoms were believed to be the smallest particles of matter, so how could something so tiny be weighed? Dalton devised a way of comparing the weights of different atoms with the weight of one atom of the lightest element, hydrogen.

> ### *"The elements, if arranged according to their atomic weights, exhibit an apparent periodicity of properties."*
> **DMITRY MENDELEYEV**
> writing in the *Journal of the Chemical Society* (London), 1889

Mercury

Magnesium

CHEMISTRY CARDS
Mendeleyev made a card for each element and wrote on it its symbol, its weight, and its physical properties. He arranged the cards in rows on a table in order of atomic weight, with the lightest first (hydrogen). This produced a pattern that repeated itself—elements that behaved in similar ways lined up vertically with each other. If an element did not fit the pattern, Mendeleyev reassessed its atomic weight. By March 1869, the table and a statement of Periodic Law were ready.

Atomic number

Atomic weight

11   23

Na

Sodium

Chemical symbol

Name of element

Chemistry card

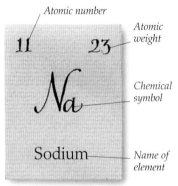

Elements lined up vertically in each column are chemically similar

Horizontal rows are called periods

MENDELEYEV'S PERIODIC TABLE
No chemistry textbook would be complete without the latest version of the Periodic Table, and there are colorful interactive versions on the Internet. The table is a quick-reference tool that provides information about each of the elements. The grid-shaped pattern devised by Mendeleyev placed them in order of atomic weight, starting with hydrogen, top left. Each element has an atomic number and he arranged them in rows so that those with similar properties lined up with each other vertically. Mendeleyev's system was not the only one available at the time, but it was exceptional in that he predicted as yet undiscovered elements, and he left spaces for them in his table in the correct positions.

MARIE CURIE (1867–1934)
Shown here working in her laboratory, Marie Curie was a world-famous scientist. She had many medals, honorary doctorates, and distinctions. and was the first female professor at the Sorbonne. She has been a remarkable role model for women, inspiring them to pursue their own careers and encouraging them to become scientists.

1867	November 7, born Manya Sklowdowska in Warsaw, Poland.
1891	Moves to France to study science in Paris.
1895	Marries Pierre Curie, professor of physics, Sorbonne University, Paris.
1898	They discover two new radioactive elements—polonium and radium.
1903	Becomes first woman in France to complete a doctorate. Receives the Nobel Prize for Physics jointly with her husband and her tutor Henri Becquerel.
1906	Pierre is killed by a horse-drawn carriage. Marie takes over his position at the Sorbonne.
1911	Awarded the Nobel Prize for Chemistry, so becomes first person to win two Nobel prizes.
1914	Becomes the head of Paris Institute of Radium. Organizes X-ray services during World War I.
1920	Creates Curie Foundation to explore radioactivity further.
1921	Goes on fundraising tour of US. Visits the White House in Washington, D.C., and receives honorary doctorate from Yale University.
1934	July 4, dies of cancer.

AN EAGER YOUNG STUDENT, Manya Sklowdowska arrived in Paris in 1891 in search of a college education that was denied her in her native Poland. She married a French physics professor, Pierre Curie, who was as idealistic and determined as herself. Their story is one of patient work, tragic setbacks, and remarkable achievements. Captivated by the mysterious rays that had just been detected in uranium, Marie and Pierre discovered two far more powerful radioactive elements—polonium and radium. After Pierre's accidental death in 1906, Marie worked on alone, bringing up their two daughters and overcoming the difficulties of being a woman working in a man's world. Not only was Marie Curie the first woman to win a Nobel Prize, but she was also the first person ever to receive two Nobel prizes.

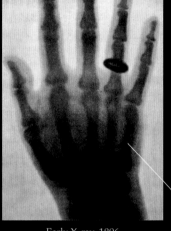

Early X-ray, 1896

A NEW KIND OF RAYS
In 1895, German professor William Röntgen (1845–1923) took the first X-ray photograph—of his wife's hand. While he was using a piece of electrical apparatus called a cathode-ray tube (p. 44), he was astonished to discover rays that could pass through flesh, but not bone or metal. Röntgen called these rays X (X meaning unknown). They later proved to be the same type of waves as light (electromagnetic). Rays of light travel in waves, but X-rays have shorter wavelengths, which gives them higher energy and enables them to penetrate softer substances.

Bones look darker because X-rays do not pass through

RADIOACTIVE ROCKS
Some substances send out invisible rays and particles that affect a photographic plate even in the dark. French physicist Henri Becquerel (1852–1908) was the first to notice this effect using uranium salts in 1896. His student Marie Curie used the term "radioactivity" to describe how energy is released when atoms disintegrate into a different form. Most atomic nuclei are stable, always having the same number of protons (positively charged particles) and neutrons (particles with no charge), but unstable ones decay, giving off alpha and beta particles, and gamma rays (high-energy light), until it loses its radioactivity, which can take millions of years.

Uranium-rich pitchblende

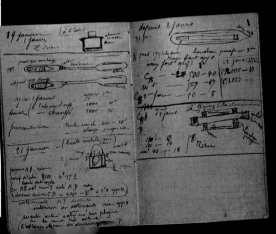

RADIOACTIVE NOTEBOOKS
Curie's radioactive substances glowed in their tubes like "faint, fairy lights." Both she and Pierre recorded their observations in notebooks such as this one. They were unaware of the danger that radiation posed to their health, although they did suffer from tiredness, cracked fingers, and burns. Marie and her daughter eventually died from cancer brought on by exposure to radiation. Marie Curie's notebooks in the Bibliothèque Nationale, Paris, are still radioactive and they carry a health warning to anyone wanting to view them.

THE CURIES' QUEST

In 1898, the Curies' discovery of polonium and radium made headline news. They worked alongside each other in a small uncomfortable shed patiently searching through large quantities of the uranium ore, pitchblende, for radioactive salts. The pitchblende was broken down into different substances that were separated until pure crystals emerged, and their properties were carefully measured. "We passed the best and happiest days of our lives," Marie wrote, "devoting our entire days to our work..."

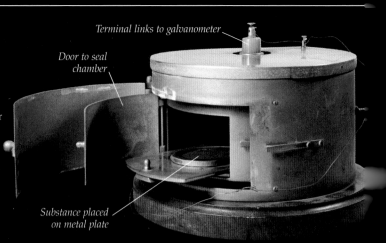

Terminal links to galvanometer

Door to seal chamber

Substance placed on metal plate

IONIZATION CHAMBER

The Curies used this sensitive piece of equipment to test radioactivity levels in different substances. The chamber contains two metal plates, and has a power supply that maintains an electric field between them. When a radioactive substance is placed on the lower metal plate, the radiation knocks out some of the electrons from the atoms, leaving charged atoms called ions. The movement of these ions forms a tiny current that can be measured with a device called a galvanometer, which detects and measures electric currrent.

"A new world opened to me, the world of science."

MARIE CURIE
on her studies in Paris, from her autobiographical notes, 1923

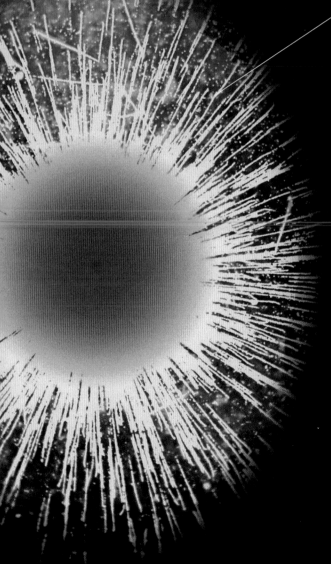

Tracks of radioactive particles emitted by radium

Dramatic colored photograph of radium salt

WAR WORK

The Curies believed knowledge should be shared and never attempted to profit from their discoveries. During World War I, Marie used the money she received from her Nobel Prize to fund mobile X-ray units, nicknamed Petites (little) Curies, and drove one to the battlefront. She trained women, including her elder daughter, Irène, shown here with Marie, as radiology assistants, to take X-rays of the wounded. The Curie Foundation, which Marie helped to set up after the war, pioneered research into cancer and its treatment using radium.

Marie Curie

Ernest Rutherford

Albert Einstein

SOLVAY CONFERENCE

In 1911, the first world conference for the revolutionary science of physics was held in Brussels, Belgium. Among those attending with Marie Curie were Albert Einstein (pp. 46–47) and Ernest Rutherford (pp. 44–45). Marie was the only woman present. This was a year of despair, when she was savagely attacked in the press about changes in her personal life, but also triumph, as she was awarded her second Nobel Prize.

Ernest Rutherford

BARON RUTHERFORD (1871–1937)
When things were going well in Rutherford's experiments, he marched around the laboratory singing "Onward Christian soldiers." He approached his work with gusto and liked simple methods that produced impressive results.

On a wall near the old Cavendish Laboratory at Cambridge University is an engraving of a crocodile by the artist Eric Gill that commemorates the forceful personality of Ernest Rutherford. He left his rural home in New Zealand to take up a research scholarship at Cambridge in 1895. Already interested in radio waves, he became absorbed in the study of radioactivity. With chemist Frederick Soddy (1877–1956), he discovered that the atoms of some elements decay into different lighter atoms and received a Nobel Prize for this in 1908. He designed brilliant experiments that probed the inner structure of the atom and produced the first nuclear reaction. By 1931, he was Baron Rutherford of Nelson, world-class scientist and motivating force in the dynamic field of nuclear physics.

1871	August 30, born at Spring Grove near Nelson, South Island, New Zealand, the fourth of 12 children.
1894	Graduates from Canterbury College, Christchurch.
1895	Becomes first research student at Cambridge University, England, not to have graduated there. Invents an electromagnetic wave detector.
1898	Reports the existence of alpha and beta rays in uranium radiation. Becomes professor of physics at McGill University, Canada.
1903	Elected fellow of the Royal Society.
1907	Becomes professor of physics at University of Manchester, England.
1908	Awarded Nobel Prize in Chemistry for his work with radioactivity.
1910	Starts investigating the inner structure of the atom, and in 1911 announces discovery of its nucleus.
1914	Knighted. Works on submarine detection during World War I.
1919	Becomes director of Cavendish Laboratory. Carries out the first artificially induced nuclear reaction.
1920	Predicts existence of the neutron.
1925	President of the Royal Society.
1931	Becomes president of the Institute of Physics for two years.
1932	Atomic nucleus split by John Cockcroft (1897–1967) and Ernest Walton (1903–1995).
1937	October 19, dies in Cambridge. Ashes are in Westminster Abbey.

CAVENDISH LABORATORY
Rutherford's room in Cambridge in 1926 looks very different to a modern high-tech laboratory, but it was home to some of the greatest discoveries in atomic science. In 1895 Rutherford came to the Cavendish Laboratory as a research student under Professor J. J. Thomson (1856–1940). He returned in 1919 to become an inspirational director, who encouraged and supported younger colleagues.

Cathode ray passes through low-pressure gas

High voltage between plates creates electric field

Heated cathode (negative pole) produces the electrons

Electrons pass through slits (positive pole)

Coils create magnetic field

Cathode-ray apparatus

Scale measure angle of beam

DISCOVERY OF SUBATOMIC PARTICLES
This apparatus has metal terminals that produce a flow of cathode rays containing electrons (particles with an negative electrical charge). It was used in 1897 by Thomson to prove atoms are not the smallest units of matter. He measured by how much a beam of rays in an electric field and then in a magnetic field were pushed to one side. The beam bent toward the positive pole so he stated it must be negatively charged and the particles must be smaller and lighter than atoms.

THE FIRST ATOM MODEL
Professor Thomson tried his particle experiments with different gases and different metals in the tube terminals that produced the cathode rays. He concluded that there are electrons in all types of matter. In 1904, he produced this model of the atom showing a number of electrons with a negative charge held together in a sphere of positive charge.

Electron

Gold foil atom's nucleus has positive charge

Most particles go straight through foil

A few alpha particles hit foil nucleus and bounce back

Some particles are deflected at an angle

FINDING THE NUCLEUS
In 1911, Rutherford published results of an experiment at McGill University, Canada. Using an apparatus called a disperser, positively charged alpha particles were fired at a piece of gold foil. Most particles passed directly through, a few were deflected at a slight angle, and a very few bounced almost directly back, pushed by a powerful force inside the gold atoms. The experiment showed that atoms are mostly empty space, but at the center there is an area of positive charge—the nucleus.

Nucleus made of protons (red) and neutrons (green)

Wire carries current through cylinder

Particles enter window

"It was almost as incredible as if you fired a 15-inch shell at a piece of tissue paper and it came back and hit you."
ERNEST RUTHERFORD
describing his particle-scattering experiment, 1909

Connecter

Copper cylinder contains low-pressure gas

Electron moves around nucleus

Screw terminal attaches to power supply

GEIGER COUNTER
Rutherford and the German physicist Hans Geiger (1882–1945) worked together at Manchester University, England, looking at the rays produced by radioactive materials. This counter is one of a number of devices Geiger designed to detect radiation. When an alpha or beta particle enters the window, it stimulates an electric current between the copper casing and a wire in its gas-filled center.

INSIDE THE ATOM
The structure of the atom was gradually pieced together to produce this model, with a central nucleus orbited (circled) by fast-moving electrons. No one could explain why electrons were not dragged to the center by the nucleus, until Danish physicist Niels Bohr (1895–1962) discovered that all electrons have different energy levels, which keeps them in fixed orbits. Within the nucleus are positively charged protons, identified by Rutherford in 1919, and neutrons, which have no charge.

Experimental advanced gas-cooled reactor produced electricity

Nuclear reactor called a pile produced fuel for weapons

Sellafield, England

Cooling towers

Nucleus has split in two

HOW THE ATOM WAS SPLIT
When Rutherford bombarded nitrogen atoms with alpha particles of radium to release protons, he converted the nitrogen into oxygen. This was the first time one element was changed into another through a process called nuclear fission. In the 1930s, physicists discovered that the heavy nuclei of radioactive uranium atoms, shown here, could be split releasing huge amounts of energy. When the nucleus splits (or fissions) into two smaller nuclei, it releases neutrons, which hit and fission further nuclei in a chain reaction.

Neutrons produced by fission

NUCLEAR POWER
The energy produced by nuclear fission was first harnessed to produce atomic weapons but, after World War II, reactors were built for electricity. Neutrons in fuel rods inside the reactor's core start to split in a chain reaction. The heat they produce is absorbed by water, creating steam that turns turbines to generate power. Here at Sellafield there are two early types of reactor, both now decommissioned.

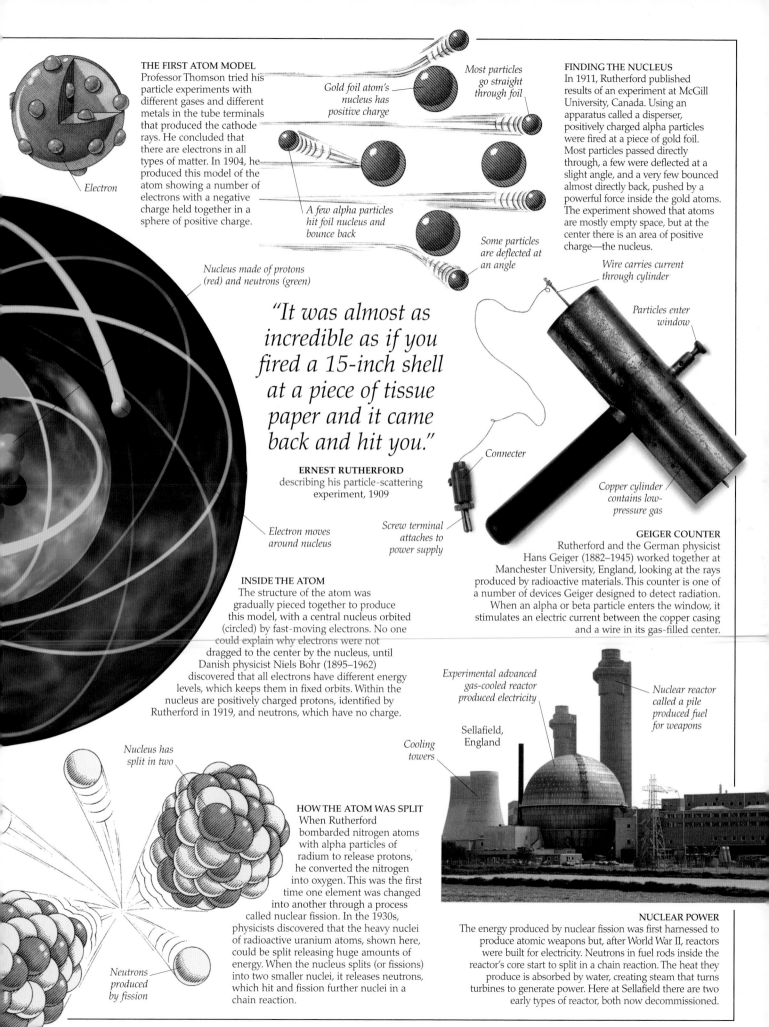

1879	March 14, born in Ulm, Germany.
1900	Awarded teaching diploma from Federal Polytechnic Institute, Zurich, Switzerland.
1902	Employed in Swiss Patent Office. In 1905 publishes articles that lay the foundations for modern physics, including Special Theory of Relativity. Formulates famous equation E=mc².
1911	Becomes Professor at Germany University, Prague, Czechoslovakia.
1912	Becomes Professor of Theoretical Physics in Zurich.
1914	Becomes Director of Kaiser Wilhelm Institute and Professor of Theoretical Physics, Berlin.
1916	Publishes General Theory of Relativity. In 1919 observation of an eclipse confirms his theory.
1921	Awarded Nobel Prize for explanation of photoelectric effect.
1933	Emigrates to the US.
1945	August 6, first atomic bomb dropped on Hiroshima.
1955	April 18, Einstein dies. His brain is saved to be examined by scientists.

Albert Einstein

WHEN GERMAN PHYSICIST Albert Einstein died in 1955, his brain was removed by a pathologist and examined. Contrary to expectations, it was the same size as that of an average person. Einstein was a mathematical genius, with a unique ability to look at the existing laws of physics and extend them in a new and revolutionary way. His ideas continue to be tested by other scientists long after he wrote them down. He predicted the energy contained within the atom and changed our understanding of how the universe works. Although Einstein was reluctant to see the atom's power harnessed in an atomic bomb, during World War II, he supported the Allies' nuclear weapons program, because he was afraid that Nazi Germany would develop its own.

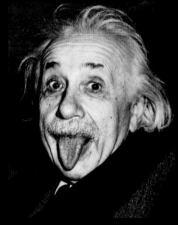

ALBERT EINSTEIN (1879–1955)
Einstein sticks out his tongue for photographers on his 72nd birthday. His theories made him a scientific superstar, traveling with his wife on world tours, and pursued by the media. A brilliant scientist in adulthood, he had a slow start, and only learned to speak fluently when he was nine. He also had a strong social conscience and campaigned vigorously for social justice and world peace.

ANNUS MIRABILIS
In 1905, when Einstein was still a junior clerk in a patent office in Bern, Switzerland, he wrote articles in his spare time with little reference to other scientific work, and sent them to the top scientific journal. The year became known as Einstein's *annus mirabilis* (Latin for wonderful year), because these ideas later transformed the world of physics. Among the papers published was his *Special Theory of Relativity*, which expanded previous knowledge about space, time, light, and matter, taking it into new, uncharted, realms.

$$"E=mc^2"$$

ALBERT EINSTEIN
Special Theory of Relativity, published
September 1905

EINSTEIN'S THEORIES
As a theoretical physicist, Einstein needed little in the way of equipment. He worked with ideas, expressing them as equations written on a blackboard or on the back of an envelope. An equation is a statement, in numbers and symbols, saying that two things are the same. Einstein's most famous equation is E=mc², which states that the energy of an object is the same as its mass times the speed of light, squared.

Blackboard used by
Einstein to deliver lecture,
December 1934

Spacecraft seems contracted when viewed from Earth

Earth seems contracted viewed from spacecraft

Viewpoint from Earth

Viewpoint from spacecraft

SPECIAL THEORY OF RELATIVITY

Isaac Newton (pp. 22–23) believed that space and time are fixed. Einstein saw that they interlinked in what he called space-time, which is related to the mass and energy of an object. The laws of physics are the same in space and on Earth and nothing can travel faster than light—a speed which does not change. How time, length, and mass are measured, however, will depend on the position and speed of movement of the person making the measurement. At ordinary speeds, on Earth for example, differences wouldn't be detectable. But if someone on Earth could see a spacecraft move through space almost the speed of light, the craft would look shorter than normal, its mass greater, and its clocks would be slower. Likewise to a spacecraft's crew, the Earth would seem contracted, and its mass larger.

EINSTEIN'S GRAVITY

For skydivers in free fall, the acceleration (increasing speed) of their fall is equal to the gravity that pulls them down to the ground. The weightlessness that they feel is similar to that of an astronaut in space. Observing this effect, which he called the equivalence principle, Einstein was able to complete his *General Theory of Relativity*. Newton (pp. 22–23) had described gravity as a force between two objects. Einstein showed that gravity is not a force as such, but is the effect of objects such as the Sun and planets, on space. Like a person sitting on a trampoline, the bulk of these large bodies curves space, causing them to fall toward each other.

A skydiver in free fall feels weightless

SUPER ENERGY

The Allies' Manhattan Project tested the first atomic bomb, code-named the Trinity Test at a desert site in New Mexico on July 16, 1945. They used a small quantity of plutonium to generate a huge amount of destructive energy. This was Einstein's equation, $E=mc^2$, in action. His equation states that the mass of an object is a measure of the energy within it. This means that mass can be converted into energy, and energy can be changed into mass. An example of this process is nuclear fission, where the energy locked up in a single atom is released in a chain reaction (p. 45).

LISA MEITNER

Talented Jewish physicist Lisa Meitner (1878–1968) fled to Sweden in 1938, when Nazi Germany took control of her native Austria. As a pioneer of nuclear fission, she realized that it could power a devastating explosive device. European scientists in the US were afraid that Hitler would be the first to create an atomic bomb. When World War II broke out in 1939 they urged Einstein to write a letter to President Franklin D. Roosevelt warning of the danger, which he did.

Massive energy released by the atomic chain reaction in the Trinity Test

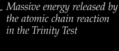

Fat Man atomic bomb

Bomb carried just over 2 lb 3 oz (1 kg) of plutonium

THE MANHATTAN PROJECT

Three nuclear weapons were built during World War II by the Manhattan Project—an international team of physicists. The team was based at a secret laboratory at Los Alamos, New Mexico. The first was launched at the test site, and the second on Hiroshima, Japan, Germany's ally, to force a surrender at the end of the war. The Fat Man bomb was detonated above Nagasaki, Japan, on August 9, 1945, killing 40,000. Einstein supported the nuclear program, but he was a pacifist, so was not asked to join the team.

Alfred Wegener

ONE OF THE MOST FUNDAMENTAL theories about the Earth came not from a geologist, but from Alfred Wegener, a German meteorologist, who studied weather patterns. In his theory of continental drift, introduced in 1915, Wegener proposed that the Earth's landmasses were once joined in a vast supercontinent, called Pangaea, until they broke free about 300 million years ago. Many scientists ridiculed this idea, but by the 1960s he was proved right. Discoveries about the ocean floor and the nature of the mantle (the hot layer around the Earth's core) provided invaluable evidence. Wegener's theory developed into the theory of plate tectonics, which explains the forces within the Earth that cause earthquakes and volcanoes, create mountain chains, and continue to move continents.

1880	November 1, Wegener born in Berlin, Germany.
1904	Awarded PhD in astronomy, Berlin University, Germany.
1906	Joins an expedition to Greenland to study polar air circulation.
1909	Starts teaching at the Marburg University, Germany.
1910	Notices that coastlines of South America and West Africa look as if they may once have been joined.
1911	Discovers fossil evidence to support his joined coastline idea.
1912	First introduces Theory of Continental Drift.
1914	Released from German army after being wounded in World War I.
1915	The Origin of Continents and Oceans is published, claiming the continents were once a single mass.
1924	Becomes professor of meteorology and Geophysics at the University of Graz, Austria.
1930	Leads a fourth expedition to Greenland, but freezes to death, November 2 or 3.

ALFRED LOTHAR WEGENER (1880–1930)
Wegener made four expeditions to Greenland. Fieldwork in the Arctic was risky, and it eventually claimed his life. After delivering supplies to a remote camp and celebrating his birthday, he died on the way back.

Launching a weather balloon

WEATHER BALLOONS
Wegener was the first to use weather balloons to track the circulation of air. In 1906 he and his brother, Kurt, established a 52-hour world record for traveling in a hot-air balloon over Germany, testing weather equipment. In 1930, members of an expedition to Greenland led by Wegener launched a balloon to check air temperature and humidity over the ice.

ARCTIC SLEDGING
Hauling sleds is backbreaking work, but tough husky dogs harnessed together in teams can pull heavy loads swiftly across the ice. When the propeller-driven sleds on Wegener's expedition foundered in deep snow, he used dog sleds to travel on a 250-mile (400-km) journey taking vital supplies to a remote inland station.

Thick coat protects dog from the cold

Husky dogs

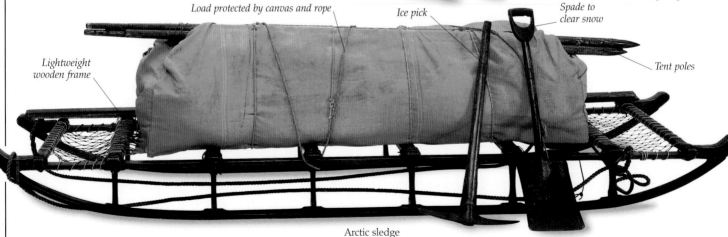

Load protected by canvas and rope

Ice pick

Spade to clear snow

Lightweight wooden frame

Tent poles

Arctic sledge

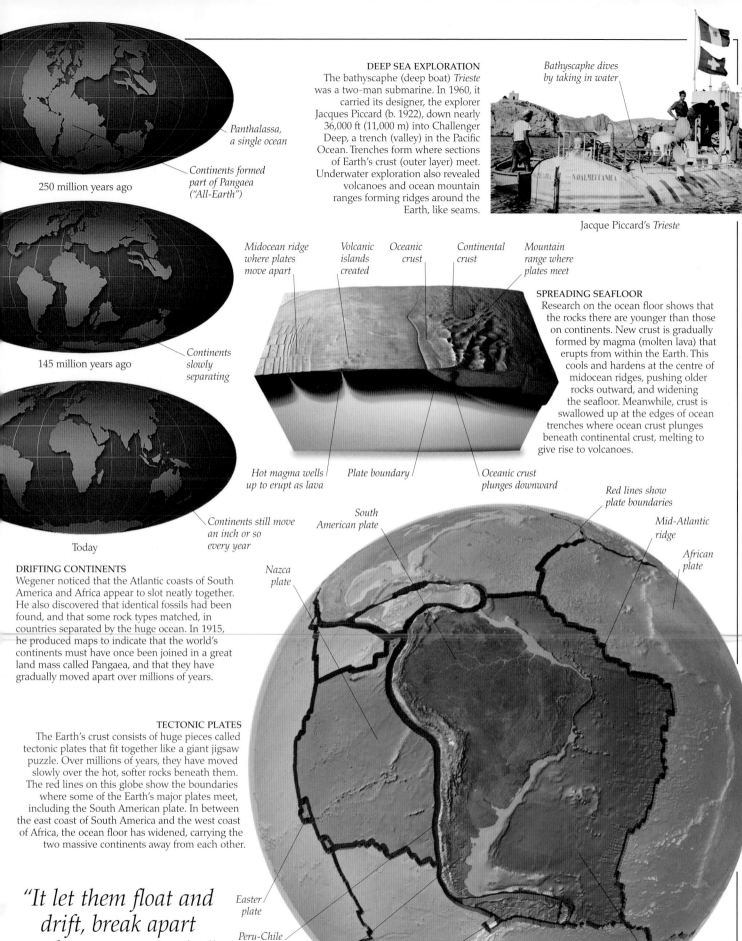

250 million years ago

Panthalassa, a single ocean

Continents formed part of Pangaea ("All-Earth")

145 million years ago

Continents slowly separating

Today

Continents still move an inch or so every year

DEEP SEA EXPLORATION
The bathyscaphe (deep boat) *Trieste* was a two-man submarine. In 1960, it carried its designer, the explorer Jacques Piccard (b. 1922), down nearly 36,000 ft (11,000 m) into Challenger Deep, a trench (valley) in the Pacific Ocean. Trenches form where sections of Earth's crust (outer layer) meet. Underwater exploration also revealed volcanoes and ocean mountain ranges forming ridges around the Earth, like seams.

Bathyscaphe dives by taking in water

Jacque Piccard's *Trieste*

Midocean ridge where plates move apart

Volcanic islands created

Oceanic crust

Continental crust

Mountain range where plates meet

SPREADING SEAFLOOR
Research on the ocean floor shows that the rocks there are younger than those on continents. New crust is gradually formed by magma (molten lava) that erupts from within the Earth. This cools and hardens at the centre of midocean ridges, pushing older rocks outward, and widening the seafloor. Meanwhile, crust is swallowed up at the edges of ocean trenches where ocean crust plunges beneath continental crust, melting to give rise to volcanoes.

Hot magma wells up to erupt as lava

Plate boundary

Oceanic crust plunges downward

Red lines show plate boundaries

Mid-Atlantic ridge

African plate

South American plate

Nazca plate

DRIFTING CONTINENTS
Wegener noticed that the Atlantic coasts of South America and Africa appear to slot neatly together. He also discovered that identical fossils had been found, and that some rock types matched, in countries separated by the huge ocean. In 1915, he produced maps to indicate that the world's continents must have once been joined in a great land mass called Pangaea, and that they have gradually moved apart over millions of years.

TECTONIC PLATES
The Earth's crust consists of huge pieces called tectonic plates that fit together like a giant jigsaw puzzle. Over millions of years, they have moved slowly over the hot, softer rocks beneath them. The red lines on this globe show the boundaries where some of the Earth's major plates meet, including the South American plate. In between the east coast of South America and the west coast of Africa, the ocean floor has widened, carrying the two massive continents away from each other.

"It let them float and drift, break apart and converge again."

HANS CLOOS, GERMAN GEOLOGIST
on Wegener's *Theory of Continental Drift*

Easter plate

Peru-Chile trench

Continental part of South American plate

Scotia plate

Ocean part of South American plate

Edwin Hubble

During the early years of the 20th century, there was a huge step forward in people's understanding of the universe. It was a time of exciting new ideas in physics, and high-tech observatories were being built, with much larger, more powerful telescopes. In 1919, an eager, young astronomer, Edwin Hubble, joined the staff at Mount Wilson Observatory, near Los Angeles. He began making careful studies of variable stars in the spiral arms of the Andromeda nebula. Nebulae are sets of stars that look like hazy clouds. Within 10 years, he had discovered that there are star systems far beyond our own system, the Milky Way, and that the universe is rapidly expanding outward.

1889	*November 20, born Marshfield, Missouri. Family later moves to Chicago.*
1910	*Receives a BSc in mathematics and astronomy from the University of Chicago. Moves to Oxford University, England, as a Rhodes Scholar, and spends three years studying for an MA in law.*
1917	*Receives a PhD from the University of Chicago's Yerkes Observatory.*
1919	*Joins the Mount Wilson Observatory, Los Angeles with its recently completed 100-in (2.5-m) Hooker reflecting telescope, the world's largest.*
1924	*Announces his discovery that there are other galaxies outside our Milky Way.*
1929	*Establishes that the universe is expanding. With Milton Humanson, formulates Hubble's Law, which helps astronomers to begin to determine the age of the universe.*
1931	*Albert Einstein visits Hubble at Mount Wilson to congratulate him on his discoveries.*
1942	*Leaves Mount Wilson to join the army during World War II, returning again after the war.*
1953	*September 28, dies of a heart attack in San Marino, California.*

EDWIN HUBBLE (1889–1953)
Hubble helped design the powerful reflector for the 200-in (5.1-m) Hale telescope at the Mount Palomar Observatory, California. He is seen here sitting inside it. The telescope became operational in 1948 and was named after the astronomer George Hale (1868–1938), founder of the Yerkes Observatory, Wisconsin, and the Mount Wilson Observatory.

VARIABLE STARS
American astronomer Henrietta Swan Leavitt (1868–1921) worked as a "computer" at Harvard College Observatory, searching photographic plates for evidence of variable stars. In 1912 she picked out Cepheid variables—stars that brighten and fade in a regular way. By examining the period over which a star's brightness varies, she devised a way of measuring distances to Cepheids. This became an invaluable tool for other astronomers, including Edwin Hubble.

Nucleus

Satellite galaxy

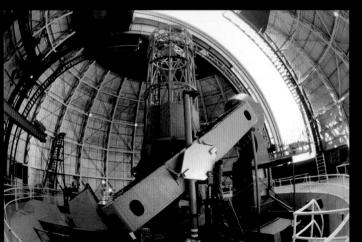

The Hooker telescope at the Mount Wilson Observatory

DISCOVERING ANDROMEDA
When Hubble was offered a job at the prestigious Mount Wilson Observatory, he jumped at the chance. Perched at 5,715 ft (1,742 m) up in the San Gabriel Mountains in Southern California, it was home to the world's two largest telescopes. In 1923, using the 100-in (2.5-m) Hooker reflector, he detected a Cepheid variable in the Andromeda nebula's spiral arms. He used this star to calculate that Andromeda was nearly a million light-years away (a figure that has since increased). Hubble also concluded that it was not just a cloud of gas, but a galaxy as vast as the Milky Way.

Spiral galaxy

Elliptical galaxy

Irregular galaxy

CLASSIFYING GALAXIES

As more galaxies were discovered, Hubble produced a system for classifying them. He divided them into broad categories based on their shapes, and arranged them in a tuning-fork pattern. Spiral galaxies (S) can be tightly wound or widely spaced. Elliptical galaxies (E) appear smooth and round, in contrast to irregular galaxies, which have no particular shape. There are also barred spirals (SB), not shown, in which the arms radiate out from a central starry band around the central nucleus.

THE HUBBLE TELESCOPE

Named after Hubble, this telescope was launched in 1990 by the space shuttle *Discovery*, and it orbits the Earth every 97 minutes, beaming back revealing images of distant galaxies. It continues Hubble's search for variable stars to determine the age of the universe. Equipped with highly sensitive equipment, the telescope is able to analyze individual wavelengths of light far more accurately than any observatory on Earth.

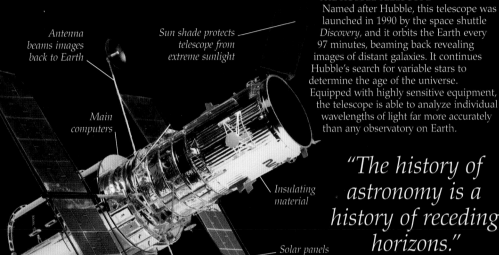

Antenna beams images back to Earth

Sun shade protects telescope from extreme sunlight

Main computers

Insulating material

Solar panels provide power

Cameras and spectrographs housed here

"The history of astronomy is a history of receding horizons."

EDWIN HUBBLE
in *The Unity of the Universe*, D.W. Schiama, 1959

Universe expanding, moving galaxies farther apart

Galaxy in early universe

Andromeda Galaxy

Early universe soon after Big Bang

Receding star

Earth

Light waves appear to lengthen as star recedes

Light waves traveling toward Earth

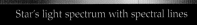

Line used to calculate shift

Star's light spectrum with spectral lines

HUBBLE'S LAW

As a star moves away from Earth, the visible light it emits shifts toward the red end of the color spectrum (known as redshift) as it gets nearer to the Earth. This is because the light waves are stretched out into longer wavelengths by the expansion of space. In 1929, Hubble and fellow astronomer Milton Humanson (1891–1972) formulated a law stating that the redshift of a galaxy is in proportion to its distance from the Earth. The farther a galaxy is from the Earth, the faster it is moving away from it.

THE UNIVERSE INFLATES

Hubble drew a graph with the speed of a galaxy along one axis (side), and the distance from Earth along the other. This enabled him to draw a line, called a "constant," that indicated that the universe is expanding at a uniform rate. The galaxies are not moving through space, but with space itself, like the galaxies drawn on these balloons. And space itself has no edge. Astronomers began to realize that not only was space expanding, but that it must have had a beginning, an event that became known as the "Big Bang."

Francis Crick and James Watson

THE NAME OF THE CHEMICAL DNA, which stands for deoxyribonucleic acid, has become a household word. In the early 1950s scientists were struggling to understand its role in the cells of living organisms. Linus Pauling (1901–94) in the US and a team in King's College, London, were close to a solution, when two outsiders, Francis Crick and James Watson, joined the field. They gathered information and built large models of the molecules (tiny chemical units) that make up DNA, until they pinpointed its exact shape. On March 4, 1953, they started assembling a spiral structure (a double helix); by March 7 it was finished; and by April 25 it was in print. They had discovered "the secret of life."

MONASTERY GARDENING

Austrian monk Gregor Mendel (1822–84) carried out painstaking work on thousands of pea plants to discover how they inherit characteristics, such as color, from their parents. He found that living things carry pairs of "factors" that determine the form of their offspring—his theory was later explained by genes. Darwin believed that characteristics from both parents merge in their offspring, but Mendel discovered that they remain separate and some are taken from each parent.

Nucleotide (three part unit with sugar, phosphates, and base)

Cell nucleus, containing chromosomes

Each chromosome divides into two identical parts before cell division

Chromosomes are linked by a centromere after division

Fine strand of DNA coiled inside chromosome

Phosphate (white section)

Bases bond to sugar backbone of the double helix

A COPYING CODE

A molecule of DNA is long and double-stranded, coiling like a spiral staircase in a double helix. DNA contains the chemical code that controls the way cells work and duplicate. Before a cell divides, its DNA reproduces itself so that each new cell will carry a copy of the code. First the two strands of the "ladder" uncoil and pull apart, splitting the rungs of paired chemical bases (T, A, C, G, shown in the key) in two. Then the chemical bases on each separate strand "zip" together with the bases of a new one forming two new, identical molecules wrapped in a package called a chromosome. The cell is then ready to divide.

Model of section of the DNA double helix

FRANCIS CRICK (1916–2004), LEFT, AND JAMES D. WATSON (b. 1928) RIGHT

Extrovert Englishman Francis Crick and impetuous young American James Watson pose for a lighthearted photograph beside their model of the DNA molecule. They described their first encounter in Cambridge, England, in September 1951 as a "meeting of minds," and together they made a dynamic team working in the Cavendish Laboratory in Cambridge. DNA was not their original area of expertise, but by using unconventional methods they overtook specialists in genetics, the study of heredity.

Adenine (A)

Guanine (G)

Thymine (T)

Cytosine (C)

Key to base colors

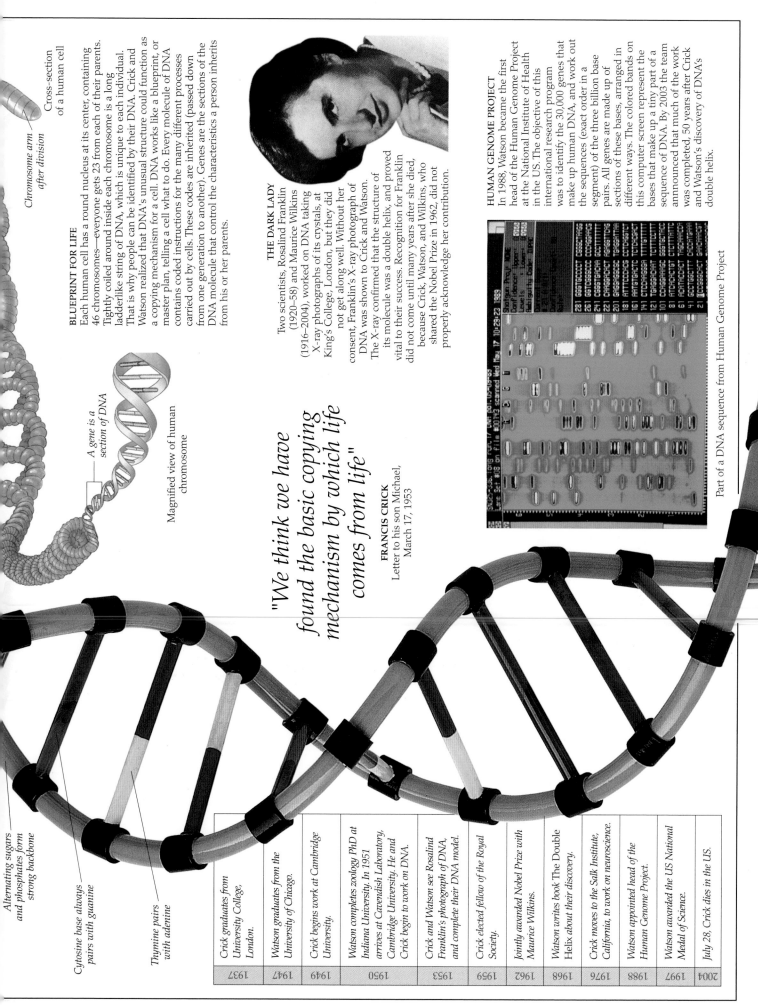

Alternating sugars and phosphates form strong backbone

Cytosine base always pairs with guanine

Thymine pairs with adenine

A gene is a section of DNA

Magnified view of human chromosome

Chromosome arm after division

Cross-section of a human cell

BLUEPRINT FOR LIFE

Each human cell has a round nucleus at its center, containing 46 chromosomes—everyone gets 23 from each of their parents. Tightly coiled around inside each chromosome is a long ladderlike string of DNA, which is unique to each individual. That is why people can be identified by their DNA. Crick and Watson realized that DNA's unusual structure could function as a copying mechanism for a cell. DNA works like a blueprint, or master plan, telling a cell what to do. Every molecule of DNA contains coded instructions for the many different processes carried out by cells. These codes are inherited (passed down from one generation to another). Genes are the sections of the DNA molecule that control the characteristics a person inherits from his or her parents.

THE DARK LADY

Two scientists, Rosalind Franklin (1920–58) and Maurice Wilkins (1916–2004), worked on DNA taking X-ray photographs of its crystals, at King's College, London, but they did not get along well. Without her consent, Franklin's X-ray photograph of DNA was shown to Crick and Watson. The X-ray confirmed that the structure of its molecule was a double helix, and proved vital to their success. Recognition for Franklin did not come until many years after she died, because Crick, Watson, and Wilkins, who shared the Nobel Prize in 1962, did not properly acknowledge her contribution.

HUMAN GENOME PROJECT

In 1988, Watson became the first head of the Human Genome Project at the National Institute of Health in the US. The objective of this international research program was to identify the 30,000 genes that make up human DNA, and work out the sequences (exact order in a segment) of the three billion base pairs. All genes are made up of sections of these bases, arranged in different ways. The colored bands on this computer screen represent the bases that make up a tiny part of a sequence of DNA. By 2003 the team announced that much of the work was completed, 50 years after Crick and Watson's discovery of DNA's double helix.

Part of a DNA sequence from Human Genome Project

"We think we have found the basic copying mechanism by which life comes from life"

FRANCIS CRICK
Letter to his son Michael, March 17, 1953

1937	Crick graduates from University College, London.
1947	Watson graduates from the University of Chicago.
1949	Crick begins work at Cambridge University.
1950	Watson completes zoology PhD at Indiana University. In 1951 arrives at Cavendish Laboratory, Cambridge University. He and Crick begin to work on DNA.
1953	Crick and Watson see Rosalind Franklin's photograph of DNA, and complete their DNA model.
1959	Crick elected fellow of the Royal Society.
1962	Jointly awarded Nobel Prize with Maurice Wilkins.
1968	Watson writes book The Double Helix about their discovery.
1976	Crick moves to the Salk Institute, California, to work on neuroscience.
1988	Watson appointed head of the Human Genome Project.
1997	Watson awarded the US National Medal of Science.
2004	July 28, Crick dies in the US.

Alan Turing

DURING WORLD WAR II, British code-breakers working at a country house called Bletchley Park, near London, decoded secret radio messages intercepted from the German army and navy. Among them was a brilliant mathematician, Alan Turing, who developed a machine that cracked the German Enigma Code. Turing's ideas about computing were well in advance of his time. He was interested in the idea of a machine, which was more flexible than a calculator and capable of working like the human mind to handle a variety of tasks. After the war, Turing worked on several large-scale computer projects, including a design for the Automated Computer Engine (ACE), Britain's first stored-program computer. By the end of the 20th century, his idea of an intelligent machine able to assist us in almost any aspect of life had become a reality—the modern computer.

ALAN TURING (1912–54)
Nicknamed "The Prof" at Bletchley Park, Turing was humorous, hardworking, and excelled at cross-country running. His team in Hut Eight successfully decoded German naval messages, saving many British ships from being sunk by German U-boats.

1912	June 23, born in London, England, the son of a member of the Indian Civil Service.
1934	Receives BA in mathematics from Cambridge University, England.
1936	Goes to Princeton University in the US. Publishes ideas for the Turing Machine—a machine that would be able to read and execute programs.
1939	September, starts at Bletchley Park the day after Britain declares war on Germany. Designs the Bombe machine with Gordon Welchman (1906–85).
1940	Solves the German naval Enigma coding system.
1945	Awarded OBE for his wartime work. Joins National Physical Laboratory, London.
1946	Presents paper on the first design for Automated Computer Engine.
1947	Moves to Manchester University, working on software for the Manchester Mark I computer.
1950	Devises the Turing Test to assess capability of a machine to carry out an intelligent conversation.
1951	Elected Fellow of the Royal Society.
1954	June 7 dies from cyanide poisoning, probably suicide.

THE BOMBE CODE-BREAKER
This took its name from the original Polish design, which dropped a part to the floor with a bang when it came up with a solution. Turing's version, was 7 ft (2.1 m) wide, 6 ft 6 in (2 m) tall, and weighed about a ton. Enigma machine rotors were put into the machine to find weaknesses in the code. They were turned through different positions by electronic signals carried along coiled wires.

GERMAN ENIGMA MACHINE
This machine encrypted (coded) and decoded German military messages. It was compact and portable. As words were keyed in, they were mixed up electronically. But the use of short repeated words or phrases gave British code-breakers using the Bombe machine a way of guessing at parts of the message. By mid-1945, over 200 Bombe machines and a staff of 2,000 operators raced to keep pace with Enigma settings that were changed on a daily basis.

3. Current received by rotors (wheels), which spin twice changing each letter six times

4. Lampboard receives final signal and coded letter lights up

Enigma rotors loaded on to spindles

1. Letter pressed on keyboard sends current to plugboard

2. Current received by plugboard, which makes one change to the letter

Wooden case

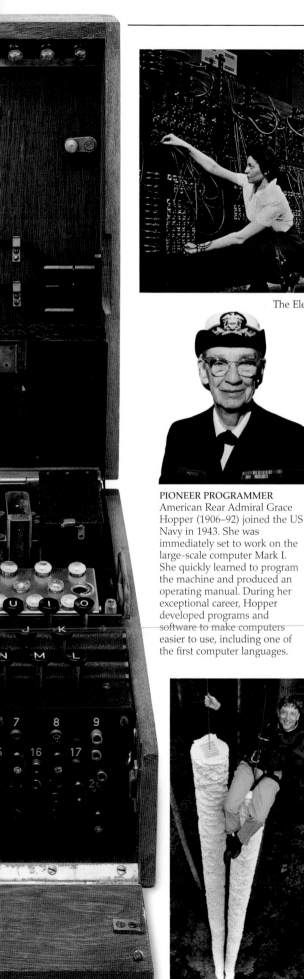

The Electronic Numerical Integrator and Computer

BIG THINKERS

Projects to develop huge electronic digital machines (processing information as numbers) gathered pace in Britain and the US in the 1940s. The Electronic Numerical Integrator and Computer (ENIAC) was completed in 1946 at the University of Pennsylvania. It was a massive 30 tons (27 metric tons), 8 ft (2.4 m) high, and 100 ft (30.5 m) long. Engineered by John Mauchly and J. Presper Eckert to calculate the paths of artillery shells, ENIAC punched its calculations on to cards, to be converted into printed data. Its circuits were so big it had 18,000 vacuum tubes (which regulated the flow of electrical current) and needed 80 air blowers to cool them.

Using an early transistor

Supporting frame

PIONEER PROGRAMMER

American Rear Admiral Grace Hopper (1906–92) joined the US Navy in 1943. She was immediately set to work on the large-scale computer Mark I. She quickly learned to program the machine and produced an operating manual. During her exceptional career, Hopper developed programs and software to make computers easier to use, including one of the first computer languages.

Block holding two pointed wire probes

Germanium crystal

THE FIRST TRANSISTOR

A transistor controls flow of electricity. This early transistor is 4 in (10 cm) high and was developed in 1947 by the American Bell Laboratory team. They had discovered that when two electrical contacts were placed on a crystal made from the element germanium, which had a current flowing through it, the current was amplified (became larger). Small transistors were essential to the development of smaller computers.

Replica of the first working transistor

HOME COMPUTERS

Bill Gates, founder of the computer company Microsoft®, demonstrates the storage capacity of a CD, by suspending himself above 330,000 sheets of paper. By the 1970s, an electrical component, a microprocessor, made it possible to produce compact, cheap, easy-to-use computers. When Gates and fellow Harvard University student Paul Allen saw an advertisement for the MITS Altair 8800, an inexpensive self-assembly microcomputer, they saw its potential for everyday use. In 1975, they dropped out of college to work on software for it, founding Microsoft®.

WORLD WIDE WEB

The internet links us to a body of information that would astound early computer pioneers. Founded by Tim Berners-Lee, the internet's World Wide Web was first devised for the particle physics laboratory at CERN, to help teams of scientists working in different places.

James Lovelock

EARTH SYSTEMS SCIENCE is the study of the whole Earth, including its biosphere (the planet's shell of land and water in which life appears), atmosphere, and geology. This way of looking at our planet as one interconnected unit owes much to writer and environmentalist James Lovelock. As a freelance scientist, he forged a career as a medical researcher, NASA space scientist, meteorologist, and geologist. A skilled inventor, he devised instruments for detecting chemicals in the Earth's atmosphere, and traces of life forms on Mars. In the 1960s Lovelock developed a theory that describes Earth as a living organism regulated by processes that maintain its suitability for life. He named this theory Gaia, after the Greek goddess of the Earth.

JAMES LOVELOCK (b. 1919)
This photograph shows Lovelock at the University of Houston, Texas, where he worked in the 1960s with scientists in NASA's Jet Propulsion Laboratory. Data collected by his instruments contributed to important discoveries about the environment.

ELECTRON CAPTURE DETECTOR
In 1957, Lovelock designed a handheld piece of equipment called the electron capture detector (ECD) to detect minute amounts of chemical pollutants in water, soil, and air. Conducting his own research, he found contamination in plants and animals, even in Antarctica. In the 1970s, research showed that some chemicals, called CFCs (chlorofluorocarbons), could destroy the ozone layer, a layer of the upper atmosphere that protects against ultraviolet rays.

Rachel Carson

"We should be the heart and mind of the Earth, not its malady."

JAMES LOVELOCK
Independent newspaper, January 16, 2006

Emperor penguin

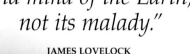

Spraying crops with pesticides

SILENT SPRING
In the 1950s American biologist Rachel Carson (1907–64) became so concerned about the use of DDT, the world's most powerful pesticide, that she spent four years collecting evidence about its dangerous effects. She used data collected with Lovelock's ECD in her research. Her book *The Silent Spring*, published in 1962, gave a compelling account of how chemicals enter the food chain. DDT was banned in the US in 1972.

1919	*July 26, Lovelock born in Letchworth Garden City, Hertfordshire, England.*
1941	*Graduates in chemistry at Manchester University, works for Medical Research Council. In 1948, awarded PhD in medicine.*
1954	*Receives Rockefeller Traveling Fellowship.*
1957	*Invents the electron capture detector (ECD).*
1961-64	*Works with Jet Propulsion Laboratory on devices for analyzing lunar soils and finding traces of life on Mars.*
1964	*Begins to work as freelance scientist and writer.*
1970	*Monitors air over coast of western Ireland, finding CFCs. Funds himself to travel to Antarctic and back by ship to continue research.*
1974	*Made a fellow of the Royal Society of London.*
1979	*Gaia: A New Look at Life on Earth is published and becomes instant classic.*
1997	*Receives the Japanese Blue Planet award.*
2006	*Publishes Revenge of Gaia sending out a rousing alarm call—the planet is sick and in danger.*

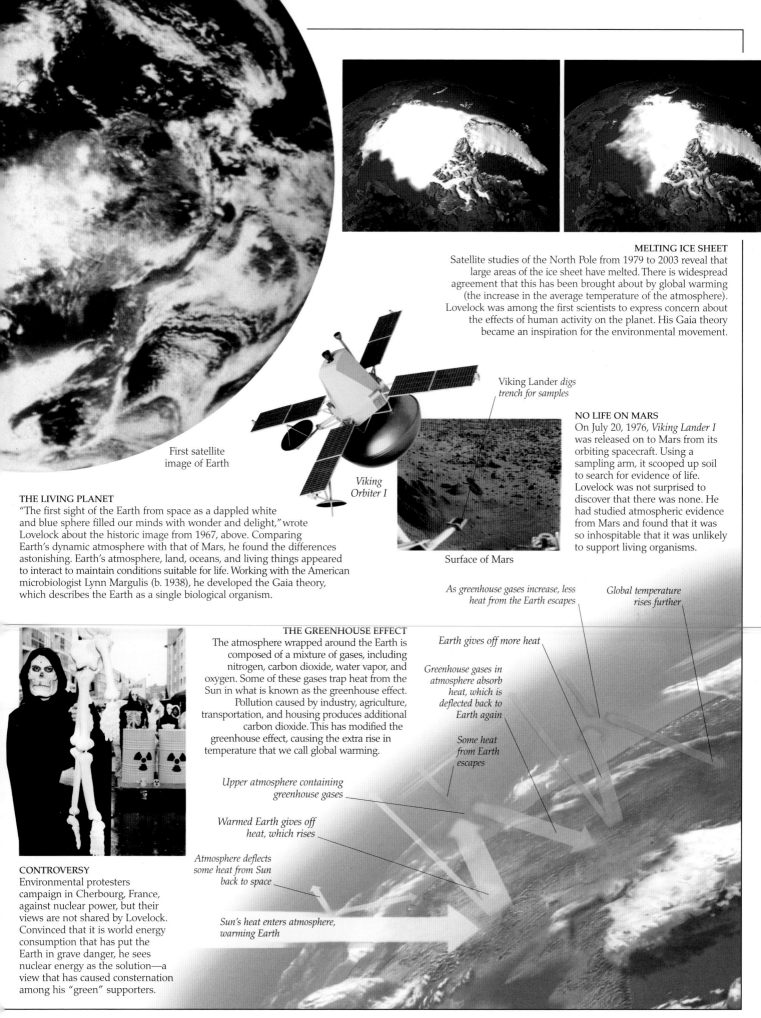

First satellite
image of Earth

MELTING ICE SHEET

Satellite studies of the North Pole from 1979 to 2003 reveal that large areas of the ice sheet have melted. There is widespread agreement that this has been brought about by global warming (the increase in the average temperature of the atmosphere). Lovelock was among the first scientists to express concern about the effects of human activity on the planet. His Gaia theory became an inspiration for the environmental movement.

*Viking Lander digs
trench for samples*

*Viking
Orbiter I*

NO LIFE ON MARS

On July 20, 1976, *Viking Lander I* was released on to Mars from its orbiting spacecraft. Using a sampling arm, it scooped up soil to search for evidence of life. Lovelock was not surprised to discover that there was none. He had studied atmospheric evidence from Mars and found that it was so inhospitable that it was unlikely to support living organisms.

Surface of Mars

THE LIVING PLANET

"The first sight of the Earth from space as a dappled white and blue sphere filled our minds with wonder and delight," wrote Lovelock about the historic image from 1967, above. Comparing Earth's dynamic atmosphere with that of Mars, he found the differences astonishing. Earth's atmosphere, land, oceans, and living things appeared to interact to maintain conditions suitable for life. Working with the American microbiologist Lynn Margulis (b. 1938), he developed the Gaia theory, which describes the Earth as a single biological organism.

*As greenhouse gases increase, less
heat from the Earth escapes*

*Global temperature
rises further*

THE GREENHOUSE EFFECT

The atmosphere wrapped around the Earth is composed of a mixture of gases, including nitrogen, carbon dioxide, water vapor, and oxygen. Some of these gases trap heat from the Sun in what is known as the greenhouse effect. Pollution caused by industry, agriculture, transportation, and housing produces additional carbon dioxide. This has modified the greenhouse effect, causing the extra rise in temperature that we call global warming.

Earth gives off more heat

*Greenhouse gases in
atmosphere absorb
heat, which is
deflected back to
Earth again*

*Some heat
from Earth
escapes*

*Upper atmosphere containing
greenhouse gases*

*Warmed Earth gives off
heat, which rises*

*Atmosphere deflects
some heat from Sun
back to space*

*Sun's heat enters atmosphere,
warming Earth*

CONTROVERSY

Environmental protesters campaign in Cherbourg, France, against nuclear power, but their views are not shared by Lovelock. Convinced that it is world energy consumption that has put the Earth in grave danger, he sees nuclear energy as the solution—a view that has caused consternation among his "green" supporters.

Dorothy Hodgkin

ENGLISH SCULPTOR HENRY MOORE met Dorothy Hodgkin in 1965 and was inspired to draw a portrait of her remarkable hands. Despite being crippled by rheumatoid arthritis (a disease that affects joints), they skillfully handled tiny crystals for many years. When Hodgkin began her career as a chemist in the 1930s, crystallography (the study of how atoms are arranged in crystals) was a new science. She trained in the technique of using X-rays to analyze crystals of important biological materials, and became a leader in her field. In 1964, she was the third woman ever to win the Nobel Prize for chemistry. Hodgkin was a committed socialist and pacifist, and she also gave enormous support to scientists around the globe.

DOROTHY CROWFOOT HODGKIN (1910–94)
This photograph was taken in the 1940s, when Dorothy Hodgkin was working on penicillin. This task took many years and she spent many hours at a laboratory bench and her computer. She had a warm personality, and inspired great affection in students and friends.

Spodumene

INSIDE CRYSTALS
A crystal is a solid made up of atoms or molecules. It has a definite shape and volume, unlike a liquid or a gas. Crystals consist of a repeated pattern of unit cells, with ions linked together in three-dimensional shapes, such as a cube or hexagon. They are found in solids, such as the minerals shown here, which occur naturally in rocks. Hodgkin loved crystals as a child, and had an analysis kit for testing stones from the stream in the yard of her childhood home in Khartoum, Sudan.

Azurite and malachite

Almandine garnet

"I was captured for life by chemistry and by crystals."

DOROTHY HODGKIN
Dorothy Hodgkin: A Life, Georgina Ferry 1998

Chrysoberyl

Rose quartz

Pattern of spots indicates crystal structure

X-ray of copper sulfate crystal

Copper sulfate crystals in a shallow dish

Camera made of brass tubing

Bernal's X-ray diffraction camera, 1920s

Clock face supports and turns crystal

BOUNCING RAYS
The atomic structure of crystals cannot be seen with an ordinary microscope, but in 1912 German physicist Max von Laue (1879–1960) produced an X-ray photograph of one. He fired the rays at a single copper sulfate crystal from different angles, causing them to diffract (scatter) as they bounced off the atoms inside. Hodgkin's tutor John Bernal improvised this early diffraction camera from an alarm clock, brass tubing, and bicycle clips. Bernal and Hodgkin were the first to produce a diffraction pattern from a crystal of biological material.

58

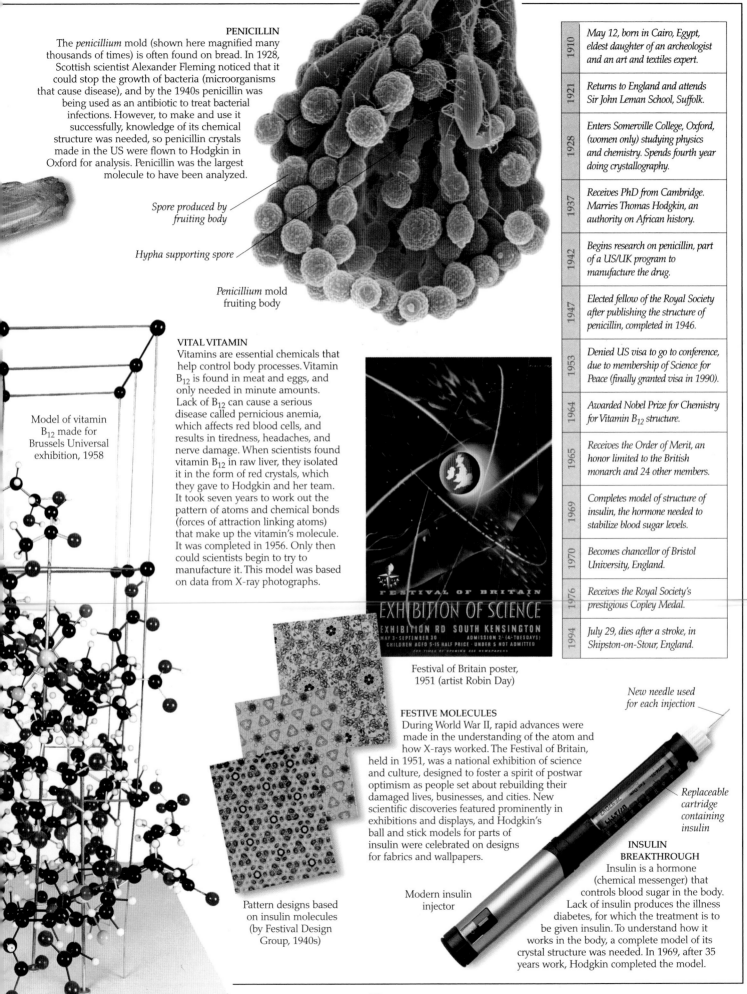

PENICILLIN

The *penicillium* mold (shown here magnified many thousands of times) is often found on bread. In 1928, Scottish scientist Alexander Fleming noticed that it could stop the growth of bacteria (microorganisms that cause disease), and by the 1940s penicillin was being used as an antibiotic to treat bacterial infections. However, to make and use it successfully, knowledge of its chemical structure was needed, so penicillin crystals made in the US were flown to Hodgkin in Oxford for analysis. Penicillin was the largest molecule to have been analyzed.

Spore produced by fruiting body

Hypha supporting spore

Penicillium mold fruiting body

1910	*May 12, born in Cairo, Egypt, eldest daughter of an archeologist and an art and textiles expert.*
1921	*Returns to England and attends Sir John Leman School, Suffolk.*
1928	*Enters Somerville College, Oxford, (women only) studying physics and chemistry. Spends fourth year doing crystallography.*
1937	*Receives PhD from Cambridge. Marries Thomas Hodgkin, an authority on African history.*
1942	*Begins research on penicillin, part of a US/UK program to manufacture the drug.*
1947	*Elected fellow of the Royal Society after publishing the structure of penicillin, completed in 1946.*
1953	*Denied US visa to go to conference, due to membership of Science for Peace (finally granted visa in 1990).*
1964	*Awarded Nobel Prize for Chemistry for Vitamin B$_{12}$ structure.*
1965	*Receives the Order of Merit, an honor limited to the British monarch and 24 other members.*
1969	*Completes model of structure of insulin, the hormone needed to stabilize blood sugar levels.*
1970	*Becomes chancellor of Bristol University, England.*
1976	*Receives the Royal Society's prestigious Copley Medal.*
1994	*July 29, dies after a stroke, in Shipston-on-Stour, England.*

VITAL VITAMIN

Vitamins are essential chemicals that help control body processes. Vitamin B$_{12}$ is found in meat and eggs, and only needed in minute amounts. Lack of B$_{12}$ can cause a serious disease called pernicious anemia, which affects red blood cells, and results in tiredness, headaches, and nerve damage. When scientists found vitamin B$_{12}$ in raw liver, they isolated it in the form of red crystals, which they gave to Hodgkin and her team. It took seven years to work out the pattern of atoms and chemical bonds (forces of attraction linking atoms) that make up the vitamin's molecule. It was completed in 1956. Only then could scientists begin to try to manufacture it. This model was based on data from X-ray photographs.

Model of vitamin B$_{12}$ made for Brussels Universal exhibition, 1958

Festival of Britain poster, 1951 (artist Robin Day)

FESTIVE MOLECULES

During World War II, rapid advances were made in the understanding of the atom and how X-rays worked. The Festival of Britain, held in 1951, was a national exhibition of science and culture, designed to foster a spirit of postwar optimism as people set about rebuilding their damaged lives, businesses, and cities. New scientific discoveries featured prominently in exhibitions and displays, and Hodgkin's ball and stick models for parts of insulin were celebrated on designs for fabrics and wallpapers.

Pattern designs based on insulin molecules (by Festival Design Group, 1940s)

New needle used for each injection

Replaceable cartridge containing insulin

Modern insulin injector

INSULIN BREAKTHROUGH

Insulin is a hormone (chemical messenger) that controls blood sugar in the body. Lack of insulin produces the illness diabetes, for which the treatment is to be given insulin. To understand how it works in the body, a complete model of its crystal structure was needed. In 1969, after 35 years work, Hodgkin completed the model.

Richard Feynman

RICHARD FEYNMAN (1918–88)
Witty and inspirational, Feynman was a brilliant scientist with a gift for communication and getting to the heart of a problem. He called his area of research the "Strange Theory of Light and Matter." He was a Nobel Prize winner, popular writer and lecturer, great practical joker, accomplished lockpicker, and he played the bongo drums.

THE FEYNMAN FAMILY CAR in the 1970s was a yellow camper van covered with squiggly drawings, and the license plate read "Quantum." Physicist Richard Feynman's area of research was quantum electrodynamics. This looks at how particles and tiny "packets" of energy (quanta), interact within the atom to produce electromagnetic radiation. Feynman's diagrams (used to decorate his car) were a code to show the interactions between these particles.

1918	May 11, born in Far Rockaway, New York, the son of Russian-Jewish immigrants.
1939	Receives BSc in mathematics from Massachusetts Institute of Technology (MIT). Becomes interested in theoretical physics and quantum mechanics (behavior of subatomic particles).
1942	Receives a PhD from Princeton, where he works on an atomic bomb project. Einstein attends Feynman's first seminar.
1943	Joins the Manhattan Project, the team working on the atomic bomb.
1945	Appointed Professor of Theoretical Physics at Cornell University.
1945	Moves to California Institute of Technology.
1965	Awarded Nobel Prize for Physics with Julian Schwinger (1918–94) and Sin-Itiro Tomonaga (1906–79).
1985	Publishes Surely You're Joking Mr. Feynman, this first best-seller.
1986	Appointed to team investigating the Challenger accident.
1988	February 15, dies of stomach cancer.

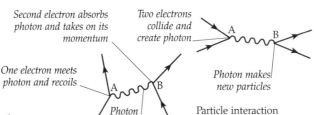

Second electron absorbs photon and takes on its momentum

Two electrons collide and create photon

One electron meets photon and recoils

Photon makes new particles

Photon exchanged by electrons

Particle interaction diagrams

FEYNMAN'S DIAGRAMS
These strange squiggles are examples of diagrams used by scientists to describe how subatomic particles can interact. Every line represents a particle. The right diagram could represent an electron (straight lines) at A kicking an electron at B out of an atom by exchanging a photon (wiggly line). The left diagram describes electrons destroying each other at A, producing a photon, and rematerializing at B as a new form of matter.

> *"All scientific knowledge is uncertain. This experience with doubt and uncertainty is important."*
>
> **RICHARD FEYNMAN**
> *The Meaning of It All*, published 1998

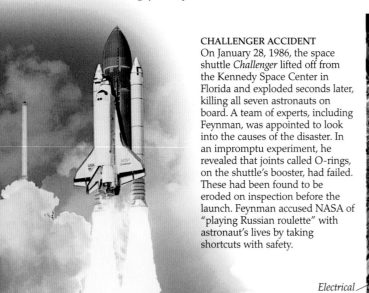

CHALLENGER ACCIDENT
On January 28, 1986, the space shuttle *Challenger* lifted off from the Kennedy Space Center in Florida and exploded seconds later, killing all seven astronauts on board. A team of experts, including Feynman, was appointed to look into the causes of the disaster. In an impromptu experiment, he revealed that joints called O-rings, on the shuttle's booster, had failed. These had been found to be eroded on inspection before the launch. Feynman accused NASA of "playing Russian roulette" with astronaut's lives by taking shortcuts with safety.

Electrical sparks from particle beam

ACCELERATING PARTICLES
Inside the atom, tiny subatomic particles dart around inside and around the nucleus. Particle physicists such as Feynman study how they interact with each other. Subatomic particles have to be released from their atoms in special chambers that smash the atoms altogther. Giant electrical sparks flash through this Particle Beam Fusion Accelerator II, in Albuquerque, New Mexico, when a particle beam of trillions of watts of power strikes its small target of gold and other elements, breaking particles away from their atoms.

Stephen Hawking

THE FRAIL FIGURE OF Stephen Hawking in his wheelchair has come to symbolize the triumph of a highly intelligent mind over matter. Despite a crippling illness, he has had an exceptional career as an astrophysicist and science communicator, exploring big ideas about black holes and how the universe began. His book *A Brief History of Time* remained on the best-seller lists for over four years. A popular science celebrity, he gives public lectures, comments on current issues, and has even appeared in *Star Trek* and *The Simpsons*.

STEPHEN HAWKING (b. 1942)
When Hawking was 21, he was diagnosed with motor neurone disease, which attacks nerve cells and causes paralysis. Against the odds, he survived. To communicate, he uses a computer that changes signals into speech with a muscle in his cheek.

1942	*January 8, born in Oxford, England.*
1962	*Receives BA from University College, Oxford, specializing in physics. Transfers to Trinity Hall, Cambridge, to study cosmology.*
1963	*Motor neurone disease diagnosed.*
1965	*Begins work on singularities (gravitational features of space-time) in Einstein's General Theory of Relativity, working for many years with Roger Penrose (b. 1931).*
1966	*Awarded a fellowship at Gonville and Caius College, Cambridge.*
1970	*Shows that black holes can emit radiation.*
1974	*Elected fellow of the Royal Society, one of the youngest ever.*
1977	*Becomes professor of gravitational physics, Cambridge, and in 1979 appointed Lucasian professor of mathematics.*
1988	*Publishes A Brief History of Time.*
2006	*Receives the Royal Society's prestigious Copley Medal.*

First galaxies form

Universe expansion slows

Almost 400,000 electrons combine with atomic nuclei to form heavier atoms

Temperature drops gradually—protons and neutrons collide forming nuclei of heavier elements within a few minutes

In a miniscule fraction of a second, protons and neutrons appear

The universe expands as particles and antiparticles that wipe each other out, at trillions of degrees Celsius

From a singularity, the universe starts, tiny, dense, hot, and full of energy, about 14 billion years ago

BIG BANG THEORY
This theory attempts to explain how the universe began. Hawking, with other physicists, looked at Einstein's *General Theory of Relativity*, and calculated that time, space, mass, and energy must have begun together. From a tiny, dense point of energy (a singularity), the universe emerged and expanded in seconds, producing particles of matter as the temperature cooled. From particles came atoms and from atoms elements came together and galaxies were formed.

BLACK HOLES
Streams of gas and dust are sucked from a large star into a glowing spiral of material around a black hole. A black hole is a small and incredibly dense body, produced by the collapse of a massive star. It has a gravitational pull so strong that light cannot escape. Until 1974 scientists believed that anything that passes the entering a black hole is destroyed. Then Hawking showed that black holes do radiate some energy in the form of particles.

Black hole surrounded by accretion disk of swirling material

THE BLACK HOLE BET
At a conference in 2004, Hawking admitted defeat in a famous bet with American scientist John Preskill. In 1974, Hawking believed that once something had been swallowed up by a black hole, no trace remained. He now agrees that information about the object leaks back into the universe. The prize was a baseball encyclopedia.

Science and the future

WHO WILL BE THE GREAT scientists of the future? Today, science embraces many different subjects, with teams of scientists working on specialized topics, using technology that would have astounded researchers just a century ago. Funding provided by governments and large organizations guides the direction of their research. In years to come, scientists will be busy seeking solutions to the problems of the world's changing climate, hunger, and disease. Discoveries are the result of the efforts of generations of scientists who have built on each other's ideas, but there is always a chance that another individual, like Einstein or Newton, will come up with an extraordinary discovery.

HOW DID LIFE BEGIN?
In the warm, shallow waters of Shark Bay, West Australia, colonies of single-celled cyanobacteria (microorganisms) form rocky mounds, called stromatolites. They trap light to make energy, in a process called photosynthesis, releasing bubbles of oxygen. Fossil stromatolites found in some of the Earth's oldest rocks indicate that they gave life-giving oxygen to the early atmosphere. Scientists studying bacteria hope to find out more about the origins of life.

FUTURE CLIMATE
One of the biggest challenges facing scientists today is global warming. Here, a glaciologist uses a long portable drill to take a sample, called a core, from deep inside a polar ice sheet. Ice cores help to measure the speed at which polar ice is forming and melting, and deep samples contain dust and bubbles that provide data about the climate long ago. Knowledge about past and present climates is used to predict what might happen in the future.

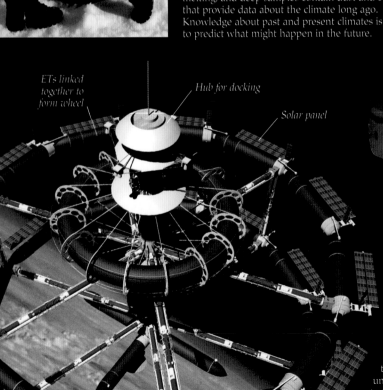

ETs linked together to form wheel

Hub for docking

Solar panel

FUTURE VACATIONS
Imagine a visit to a luxury hotel in space, with artificial gravity, air-conditioning, and views that are out of this world. Commercial companies have been designing space hotels for years, but cost has been an obstacle to creating them. This model proposes to recycle the external tanks (ETs) of the space shuttle to form a ring of units. With advances in technology, people could soon start taking vacations in space.

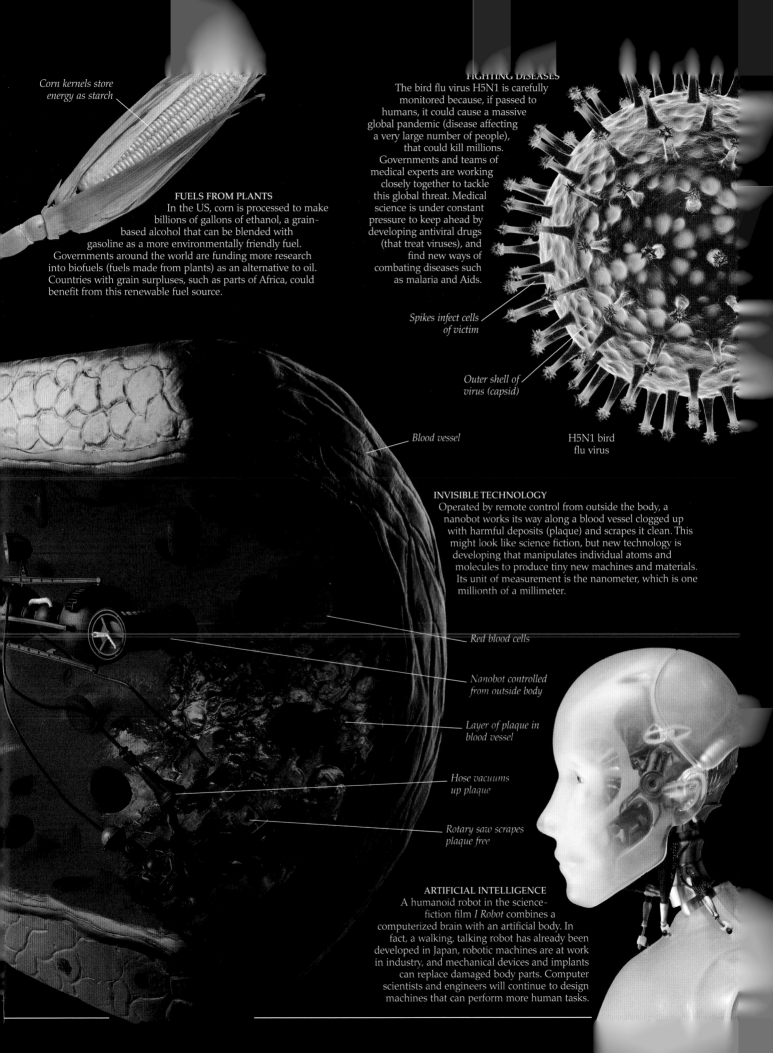

Corn kernels store
energy as starch

FUELS FROM PLANTS
In the US, corn is processed to make
billions of gallons of ethanol, a grain-
based alcohol that can be blended with
gasoline as a more environmentally friendly fuel.
Governments around the world are funding more research
into biofuels (fuels made from plants) as an alternative to oil.
Countries with grain surpluses, such as parts of Africa, could
benefit from this renewable fuel source.

FIGHTING DISEASES
The bird flu virus H5N1 is carefully
monitored because, if passed to
humans, it could cause a massive
global pandemic (disease affecting
a very large number of people),
that could kill millions.
Governments and teams of
medical experts are working
closely together to tackle
this global threat. Medical
science is under constant
pressure to keep ahead by
developing antiviral drugs
(that treat viruses), and
find new ways of
combating diseases such
as malaria and Aids.

Spikes infect cells
of victim

Outer shell of
virus (capsid)

H5N1 bird
flu virus

Blood vessel

INVISIBLE TECHNOLOGY
Operated by remote control from outside the body, a
nanobot works its way along a blood vessel clogged up
with harmful deposits (plaque) and scrapes it clean. This
might look like science fiction, but new technology is
developing that manipulates individual atoms and
molecules to produce tiny new machines and materials.
Its unit of measurement is the nanometer, which is one
millionth of a millimeter.

Red blood cells

Nanobot controlled
from outside body

Layer of plaque in
blood vessel

Hose vacuums
up plaque

Rotary saw scrapes
plaque free

ARTIFICIAL INTELLIGENCE
A humanoid robot in the science-
fiction film *I Robot* combines a
computerized brain with an artificial body. In
fact, a walking, talking robot has already been
developed in Japan, robotic machines are at work
in industry, and mechanical devices and implants
can replace damaged body parts. Computer
scientists and engineers will continue to design
machines that can perform more human tasks.

Milestones in science

At its most fundamental, science is simply understanding how the universe works. As such, science is as old as humankind itself. Our early ancestors tried to explain the world around them, although the explanations they produced, often spiritual, religious, or magical, would not be considered scientific today. Since those early beginnings remarkable progress has been made, and listed here are just a few of the key discoveries and inventions in the continuing story of science.

Astrolabe C. 550 CE

781 BCE Chinese astronomers make the first recorded observation of a solar eclipse.

C. 470–370 BCE Greek philosopher Democritus puts forward an early atomic theory, according to which everything consists of atoms.

384–322 BCE Greek philosopher Aristotle (p. 6) introduces the idea of systematic observation and deductive reasoning as cornerstones of scientific investigation.

C. 300 BCE Greek mathematician Euclid produces his book *Elements*, which sets out the fundamentals of the branch of mathematics called geometry.

287 BCE Sicilian mathematician Archimedes (p. 8) discovers the hydrostatic principle now named after him.

C. 250 BCE Greek astronomer and mathematician Eratosthenes makes the first accurate calculation of the Earth's circumference.

132 CE Chinese astronomer and mathematician Zhang Heng (p. 10) invents the seismometer (a device that detects earthquakes).

C. 550 CE Arab astronomers develop the astrolabe, which shows the position of the Sun and stars and tells the time.

C. 965-C. 1040 CE Persian philosopher Alhazen (p. 12) makes fundamental contributions to physics, mathematics, medicine, and particularly the study of optics.

1267 CE English Franciscan friar Roger Bacon (p. 14) compiles his great book *Opus Majus* setting out his thoughts on physics, mathematics, grammar, and philosophy.

1543 CE Polish astronomer Nicolaus Copernicus (p. 16) publishes his theory that the Sun is the center of the solar system. The Italian anatomist Andreas Vesalius (p. 18) publishes detailed, accurate illustrations of human anatomy.

C. 1595 CE Dutch optician Zacharias Janssen and his father Hans Janssen produce the first compound microscope (one that consists of more than one lens).

1600 English physician William Gilbert establishes that the Earth acts like a giant magnet.

1604 Italian mathematician Galileo Galilei (p. 16) develops his law of falling bodies, which proves that all objects fall at the same speed, irrespective of size.

1608 Dutch optician Hans Lippershey patents a type of refracting telescope (one that only uses a lens, not mirrors).

1609 German astronomer Johannes Kepler (p. 23) puts forward first two laws of planetary motion. He formulates his third law in 1619.

1616 English physician William Harvey (p. 18) announces his discovery of blood circulation.

1644 Italian physicist Evangelista Torricelli invents the mercury barometer (an instrument to measure pressure).

1662 Irish chemist Robert Boyle (p. 20) discovers a fundamental gas law, which became known as Boyle's Law.

1674 Dutch microscopist Antoni van Leeuwenhoek is the first to observe red blood cells and microorganisms.

1678 English inventor and architect Robert Hooke (p. 20) establishes the relationship between tension and stretch, now called Hooke's law.

1680 English astronomer Edmond Halley correctly predicts the return of the comet that is now named after him.

1687 English mathematician and experimenter Isaac Newton (p. 22) publishes his great book on gravity and mechanics, *Principia Mathematica*.

1690 Dutch physicist Christiaan Huygens publishes his wave theory of light.

Red blood cells

1714 German physicist Gabriel Daniel Fahrenheit produces the first accurate mercury thermometer.

1735 Swedish naturalist Carl Linnaeus (p. 28) publishes his system for classifying living things, which is still used today; his naming system is published in 1749.

1738 Swiss mathematician Daniel Bernoulli establishes the basic law of moving fluids that is now named after him.

1752 American philosopher and inventor Benjamin Franklin (p. 26) demonstrates that lightning is a natural form of electricity.

1771 English botanist Joseph Banks (p. 28) returns from a three-year voyage as botanist on HMB *Endeavour* with information on plants and animals unknown in Europe.

1774 English chemist Joseph Priestley (p. 25) discovers oxygen but calls it phlogiston.

1778 French chemist Antoine-Laurent Lavoisier (p. 24) names oxygen.

1781 English astronomer William Herschel discovers the planet Uranus.

1785 Scottish geologist James Hutton publishes *A Theory of the Earth*. His ideas form the basis of modern geology. The French physicist Charles Augustin de Coulomb discovers the law of electrostatics named after him.

1796 French naturalist Georges Cuvier publishes a paper comparing teeth of a fossil mammoth and modern elephant. Announces that mammoths are extinct.

C. 1796 English physician Edward Jenner performs the first successful vaccination, against smallpox.

1798 English man of science Henry Cavendish makes the first accurate calculation of average density of Earth.

1800 Italian physicist Alessandro Volta (p. 27) invents the first battery, known as the voltaic pile.

1801 German physicist Johann Ritter discovers ultraviolet radiation.

1805 French chemist Joseph Louis Gay-Lussac discovers the chemical composition of water.

1808 English chemist John Dalton outlines the modern atomic theory of chemistry.

1811 Italian scientist Amedeo Avogadro formulates a fundamental law of physics now known as Avogadro's Law, which states that volumes (amounts) of gas at the same pressure and temperature will always have the same number of molecules.

1820 Danish physicist Hans Christian Oersted showed that electric currents affect magnets (p. 36).
The French physicist André Ampère develops Oersted's work to establish electrodynamics.

1827 Scottish biologist Robert Brown discovers the motion of particles in a liquid, later called Brownian motion.
The German physicist Georg Simon Ohm discovers a basic law of electricity now known as Ohm's Law.

1830 Scottish geologist Charles Lyell (p. 33) publishes *Principles of Geology*, which helped establish uniformitarianism (that the present is the key to the past) as a geological concept.

1831 English scientist Michael Faraday (p. 36) discovered electromagnetic induction—the principle on which electric motors and dynamos work.

1833 English mathematician Charles Babbage (p. 34) produces his design for a programmable mechanical computer, the Analytical Engine.

Wires being connected to a voltaic pile—the earliest form of battery

1837 Swiss-American scientist Louis Agassiz develops the theory of ice ages.

1839 German physiologist Theodor Schwann establishes the cell theory of organisms.

1843 English physicist James Joule proves that heat is a form of energy. The term joule used as a SI (Standard Internationale) unit of energy is named after him.

1846 German astronomer Johann Galle discovers the planet Neptune.

1847 German scientist Hermann von Helmholtz formulates the conservation of energy law—that energy can neither be created nor destroyed.

1848 Scottish physicist William Thomson (Lord Kelvin) proposes the temperature scale now known as the Kelvin Scale.

1849 French physicist Armand Fizeau first measures the speed of light.

1850 German physicist Rudolf Clausius establishes the laws of thermodynamics.

1851 French physicist Jean Leon Foucault proves that the Earth rotates.

1856 French chemist Louis Pasteur (p. 38) proves fermentation (changing of substance into alcohol) is caused by microorganisms.

1859 English naturalist Charles Darwin (p. 32) publishes his book *The Origin of Species by Means of Natural Selection*, which forms the basis of modern evolutionary theory.

1864 Scottish physicist James Clerk Maxwell publishes the basic equations of electromagnetism.

1865 Austrian monk Gregor Mendel puts forward the basic laws of biological inheritance, later explained by genes.
Louis Pasteur (p. 38) patents the method of heat treatment to preserve foods, now known as pasteurization.

Neptune, discovered in 1846

1867 English surgeon Joseph Lister introduces antiseptic surgery.

1869 Russian chemist Dmitry Mendeleyev (p. 40) produces the first effective version of the modern Periodic Table of Elements.

1873 Scottish physicist James Clerk Maxwell proves that light consists of electromagnetic waves.

1876 German bacteriologist Robert Koch (p. 39) proves that bacillus (rod-shaped type of bacteria) causes anthrax. Scottish-American inventor Alexander Graham Bell invents the telephone.

1879 US inventor and entrepeneur Thomas Edison (p. 37) and his research team develop the commercial electric lightbulb.

1884 French chemist Henri Louis Le Châtelier identifies a key principle of equilibrium reactions (chemical changes that are reversible).

1887 German physicist Heinrich Hertz sends first radio waves.

1891 German bacteriologist Paul Ehrlich shows that antibodies help to provide immunity from disease.

1895 German physicist Wilhelm Röntgen (p. 42) discovers X-rays.

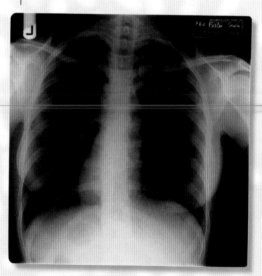

X-rays were first discovered in 1895

1896 French physicist Antoine Henri Becquerel (p. 42) discovers radioactivity.

1897 English physicist Professor J.J. Thomson (p. 44) discovers the electron.

1898 Polish chemist Marie Curie (p. 42) and her husband Pierre (a French physicist) announce their discovery of the radioactive elements radium and polonium.
New Zealand physicist Ernest Rutherford (p. 44) identifies alpha rays and beta rays.

Timeline continues on page 66

1905 German-born physicist Albert Einstein (p. 46) publishes his *Special Theory of Relativity*. He also formulates his famous equation $E=mc^2$ (that the energy of an object is equal to its mass times the speed of light squared).

1907 US geneticist Thomas Hunt Morgan proves that genes are carried on chromosomes and are the physical basis of inheritance, then begins many years work.

1911 New Zealand physicist Ernest Rutherford (p. 44) produces his "solar system" theory of atomic structure. Dutch physicist Heike Kamerlingh Onnes discovers superconductivity (an electrical circuit with no resistance).

1912 German meteorologist Alfred Wegener (p. 48) first introduces his continental drift theory (that the Earth's continents are slowly moving on giant tectonic plates).

1913 English chemist Frederick Soddy discovers isotopes (molecules of the same element that can have different weights). The Danish physicist Neils Bohr (p. 45) produces a different theory of atomic structure, now known as the quantum model.

1916 German-born physicist Albert Einstein (p. 46) publishes his *General Theory of Relativity*. Einstein renounces his German nationality.

1919 New Zealand physicist Ernest Rutherford (p. 44) first splits the atom.

1924 Austrian-Swiss physicist Wolfgang Pauli formulates his exclusion principle—that no two electrons in an atom can exist in exactly the same quantum state.

1927 German physicist Werner Heisenberg develops his uncertainty principle—that it is never possible to know both the exact position and the exact momentum of a subatomic particle.

1928 Scottish bacteriologist Alexander Fleming discovers penicillin, later used to develop antibiotic medicines.

Bacteria being destroyed by penicillin, first used on patients in the 1940s

DNA model first made in 1953

1929 US astronomer Edwin Hubble (p. 50) develops Hubble's Law, which describes the expansion of the universe.

1931 US chemist Linus Pauling puts forward a new theory of chemical bonding (how chemical elements are linked).

1932 English physicist James Chadwick discovers the neutron (one of two particles that make up the nucleus of an atom, the other being the proton).

1935 US scientists Charles Richter and Beno Gutenberg produce the scale of earthquake severity now known as the Richter scale.
The Austrian physicist Erwin Schrödinger puts forward his equation describing the wave-like properties of subatomic particles. In 1933 he developed his "Schrödinger's cat" thought-experiment to illustrate his equation.

1936 English mathematician Alan Turing (p. 54) publishes his idea for Turing machine. His theories provided an important basis for modern computing.

1940–53 US geneticist Barbara McClintock (p. 69) develops her theories about gene movements and regulation—before the DNA model that explained genes was completed by Crick and Watson.

1949 US particle physicist Richard Feynman (p. 60) introduces "Feynman diagrams" to illustrate interactions that take place between subatomic particles.

1950 English physicist Paul Dirac proposes string theory—that subatomic particles are assumed to be one dimensional "strings" rather than zero dimensional points, or dots.

1953 English biologist Francis Crick and US biologist James Watson (p. 52) complete the double-helix DNA (deoxyribonucleic acid) model and publish it.

1956 English crystallographer Dorothy Hodgkin (p. 58) discovers the structure of vitamin B_{12} using computer-aided X-ray crystallography.

1958 US electrical engineer Jack St. Clair Kilby invents the microchip.

1960 US physicist Theodore Maiman constructs the first laser.

1964 US physicists George Zweig Murray Gell-Mann propose existence of quarks (elementary subatomic particles).

Microchips invented in 1958

1967 English astronomers Jocelyn Bell and Antony Hewish discover pulsars (pulsating stars).

1968 US biochemists Har Gobind Khorana, Robert Holley, and Marshall Nirenberg receive a Nobel Prize for interpreting the genetic code of living matter that has DNA.

1974 English astrophysicist Stephen Hawking (p. 61) calculates that black holes do radiate some energy in the form of subatomic particles.

1979 English scientist James Lovelock (p. 56) publishes his book on the Gaia theory, *Gaia A New Look at Life on Earth*.

1995 Scientists at CERN in Switzerland, the world's largest particle physics laboratory prove the existence of antimattter (identical particles to particles in matter with an opposite electric charge).

1996 A team led by the English scientist Ian Wilmut produces the first successful clone of a mammal from an adult cell: Dolly the Sheep.

1998 US scientists Andrew Fire and Craig Mello publish their discovery of RNA (ribonucleic acid) interference (that messages sent from a cell in the creation of a protein by DNA can be disrupted, or changed).

2003 The completion of the Human Genome Project is announced—identifying all the genes in human DNA.

Sheep are cloned in 1996

Find out more

SCIENTISTS ARE CONTINUALLY MAKING exciting new discoveries and so there is always more to learn. Television, science magazines, science websites, museums, and exhibitions can all help you find out about the latest advances—what they are, how they might change our lives, and the people and stories behind them. But science is not just something professional scientists do. You can also do it yourself by, for instance, observing the night sky or studying nature; you might even make a new discovery yourself.

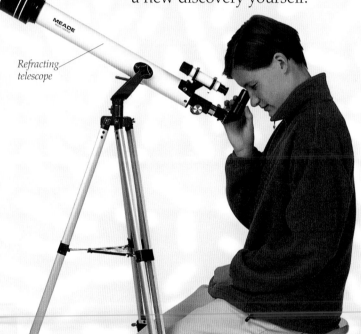

Refracting telescope

USEFUL WEBSITES

The following are general or museum websites to help you find out more about scientists.
- Information about scientists and their discoveries
  www.wikipedia.org
- Information about Nobel prizes and the prizewinners
  nobelprize.org
- Explanations of scientific principles and inventions
  www.howstuffworks.com
- Children's website for information space science
  kids.msfc. nasa.gov
- Useful source of information about Earth sciences
  www.nationalgeographic. com
- The American Museum of Natural History, New York City
  www.amnh.org
- The Smithsonian Museums, Washington, D.C.
  www.si.edu
- The Museum of Science and Industry, Chicago
  www.msichicago.org
- The Science Museum, London, UK
  www.sciencemuseum.org.uk
- The Natural History Museum, London, UK
  www.nhm.ac. uk
- The Royal Observatory, Greenwich, UK
  www.rog.nmm.ac. uk
- The Museum of the History of Science, Oxford, UK
  www.mhs.ox.ac. uk
- Whipple Museum of the History of Science, University of Cambridge, UK.
  www.hps.cam.ac. uk

LOOKING AT THE NIGHT SKY

With a telescope, binoculars, or even just your own eyes, you can see a huge variety of celestial objects, such as stars and constellations, planets, the Moon, meteors, and comets. The telescope that Galileo used to discover four of Jupiter's moons was small and primitive. With a modern amateur telescope you should be able to see what he saw and more. Also, professional astronomers cannot observe the entire sky and it is still possible to make an original discovery yourself—many comets for example, were first spotted by amateur astronomers.

Fossil of *Coelosaurus*, State Museum of Nature, Stuttgart, Germany

Walk-through heart, Museum of Science and Industry, Chicago

INTERACTIVE EXHIBITS

Many museums have exciting interactive exhibits, such as this giant walk-through model of the human heart (left). Some museums also have interactive computer activities as well as working reconstructions of original inventions and scientific experiments. These are a good way of finding out how scientists made their discoveries and how science is actually done.

VISITING MUSEUMS

There are many museums specializing in science, technology, or natural history, and visiting them is a good way to find out more about the subjects themselves and about the scientists who made important contributions. Most museums have their own websites, which usually give information about their permanent exhibits and any special exhibitions. It is a good idea to look at the website first to plan your visit.

The Nobel Prize

THIS PRIZE IS THE MOST FAMOUS of the international science awards. There are three science prizes, for physics, chemistry, and physiology or medicine, awarded every year to people who have made outstanding contributions in these fields. They were instituted by Swedish chemist and industrialist Alfred Nobel (1833–96), who made a fortune from his invention of dynamite and left much of his wealth to fund them. Nobel prizes are also given for literature, peace, and economics, although the economics prize was not stipulated by Nobel. The prizes were first awarded in 1901, since then 513 people have won science prizes.

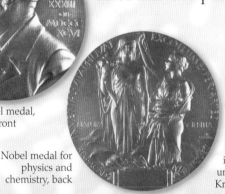

Nobel medal, front

Nobel medal for physics and chemistry, back

THE PRIZES
Those who win a Nobel Prize receive a gold medal, a Nobel diploma, and a sum of money. The medals all have a portrait of Alfred Nobel on the front, but different designs on the back, depending on what the prize is for. The prize money is given in Swedish Kronor. The amount for an unshared prize in 2006 was 10 million Kronor (about $1.4 million).

PAVLOVIAN CONDITIONING
The Russian physiologist Ivan Pavlov (1849–1936) was awarded the 1904 Nobel Prize for Physiology or Medicine, for his work on digestion. However, he is best known for his experiments on automatic reflexes (actions without thinking). In his experiments, he showed that if a bell is rung whenever a dog is fed, eventually the dog starts to drool at the sound of the bell alone. Pavlov called this response a conditioned, or acquired, reflex.

THE CEREMONY
Nobel prizes are awarded annually at ceremonies held on December 10—the anniversary of Alfred Nobel's death. The Nobel Peace Prize ceremony is held in Oslo, and is awarded by the chairman of the Norwegian Nobel Committee in the presence of the king of Norway. The other prizes are presented by the king of Sweden in the Stockholm Concert Hall. Each prizewinner (known as a Nobel Laureate) also delivers a lecture, usually several days before the award ceremony.

NOBEL RECORDS

 YOUNGEST MAN
British physicist William Lawrence Bragg (1890–1971) became the youngest man to receive a Nobel Prize when, at the age of 25, he was awarded the 1915 Nobel Prize for Physics work on analyzing crystal structures, with his father, W. Henry Bragg (1862–1942).

 YOUNGEST WOMAN
Marie Curie (pp. 42–43) was the youngest woman to receive a Nobel Prize when, aged 36, she was awarded the 1903 Physics Prize with her husband Pierre Curie and Antoine Henri Becquerel. She was also the first woman to win a prize, and is the only woman ever to have won more than one.

 OLDEST PERSON
At 87, US physicist Raymond Davis Jr. (1914–2006) is the oldest to receive an award—the 2002 Physics Prize.

MOST AWARDED FAMILY
The Curies and Joliots have together won three Nobel prizes. Marie Curie and her husband Pierre shared the 1903 Physics Prize (with Becquerel); Marie Curie won the 1911 Chemistry Prize; and her daughter Irène (1897–1956) and her husband Frédéric Joliot (1900–58) were awarded the 1935 Chemistry Prize.

FIRST NON-WESTERN SCIENTIST
Indian physicist Chandrasekhara Venkata Raman (1888–1970) was the first non-Western scientist to be awarded a Nobel Prize.

 MULTIPLE AWARDS
US chemist Linus Pauling (1901–94) is the only person to have won two unshared Nobel prizes.

Chandrasekhara Venkata Raman won the 1930 Nobel Prize for Physics

HOT RODS
When a metal rod is heated, it glows red, then gradually changes color as it gets hotter, eventually becoming white hot. This happens because the heat causes atoms in the rod to emit quanta ("packets") of electromagnetic radiation. As the rod gets hotter, the quanta become more energetic and their frequency increases, which is why the color of the glowing rod changes. This way of looking at energy as quanta was put forward by the German physicist Max Planck (1858–1947). It revolutionized physics and won him the 1918 Nobel Prize.

Red-hot iron

TRANSISTOR REVOLUTION
Almost all electronic devices now use transistors to control the flow of electricity. The first practical transistor was made in 1947 by US Bell Laboratory physicists William Shockley (1910–89), John Bardeen (1908–91), and Walter Brattain (1902–87). They shared the 1956 Nobel Prize for Physics for their work on transistors and semiconductors. Transistors are now so small that thousands can be packed on to one microchip.

Early transistor used in a high-frequency analog circuit

JUMPING GENES
The US geneticist Barbara McClintock (1902–92) discovered that the variegated color of multicolored corncobs is caused by genetic (inherited) elements that move between or within their chromosomes. This was a remarkable discovery because she made it between 1940 and 1953, before the genetic code and structure of DNA were made by Francis Crick and James Watson (pp. 52–53). McClintock was awarded the 1983 Nobel for Physiology or Medicine for her discovery. Since then movable genes (as these genetic elements are now known to be) have been found in many organisms.

PRIZE-WINNING PARTICLES
The French physicist Georges Charpak (b. 1924) won the 1992 Nobel Prize for Physics for his invention and development of particle detectors, and in particular for his invention of the multiwire chamber in 1968. This chamber was significantly more sensitive than previous detectors and was used to discover new types of subatomic particles, such as the charm quark in 1974, the discovery of which resulted in the awarding of the 1976 Nobel Prize for Physics to US physicists Burton Richter (b. 1931) and Samuel Chao Chung Ting (b. 1936).

Multicolored corncob

Particle drift chamber, CERN laboratory, Switzerland

Glossary

ALCHEMY An early type of chemistry. Its main goals were to find a way of changing metals into gold, discovering a cure for all diseases, and the secret of living forever.

ALPHA RAYS A type of radiation consisting of a stream of alpha particles, each of which is made up of two protons joined to two neutrons. Alpha particles are given off by some radioactive substances.

ASTROLABE An early astronomical instrument used to show the positions of planets and bright stars.

ATOM The smallest particle of an element that can exist on its own and take part in a chemical reaction; it is the basic unit of matter. An atom consists of a central nucleus (itself made up of protons and neutrons) surrounded by electrons.

ATOMIC BOMB A nuclear weapon that uses nuclear fission (splitting of atomic nuclei) to provide power. The other main type of nuclear weapon is the hydrogen bomb, or thermonuclear bomb, which works by nuclear fusion (joining together of atomic nuclei).

BACTERIA Microscopic single-celled organisms, probably best known for causing diseases, but also important for helping decomposition and recycling of substances.

BLACK HOLE An area of space that is so dense and has such strong gravity that nothing can escape, not even light.

CEPHEID STAR Also called a Cepheid variable, this is a type of star that pulsates and changes in brightness with precise regularity.

CHAIN REACTION A chemical or nuclear reaction that keeps itself going because the products of the reaction cause further reactions.

CHEMICAL EQUATION A shorthand way of describing a chemical reaction, using symbols to represent the substances involved.

CHEMICAL REACTION Any process in which the atoms of substances rearrange themselves to form different substances.

CHROMOSOME A thread- or rodlike structure in the nucleus of a cell that carries the cell's genes. Each species of plant and animal has a constant number; humans have 46 chromosomes (23 from each parent).

CIRCUIT A closed loop of electrical or electronic components linked so that electric current can flow around the loop.

CIRCULATION The orderly movement of fluid around a closed circuit or in an enclosed space. It is most often used to refer to the movement of blood around the body.

COMPOUND A substance that consists of two or more elements chemically linked together. For example, salt (sodium chloride) is a compound made up of sodium and chlorine.

CONDUCTOR A material that allows electricity or heat to flow through it easily. Most materials that conduct electricity well are also good conductors of heat.

ELECTRIC CHARGE The property of some particles that makes them attracted to or repelled by others. There are two types of electric charge, negative and positive. Each atom has the same number of negatively charged electrons and positively charged protons. If the atoms gain electrons, the object is negatively charged; if the atom loses electrons, it then becomes positively charged.

ELECTRIC CURRENT The flow of electric charge through a substance or around an electrical circuit.

ELECTROCHEMICAL A word used to describe a process that involves both electrical and chemical changes. For example, a battery is an electrochemical device because it uses a chemical reaction to produce electricity.

Chemical reaction

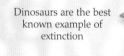

Dinosaurs are the best known example of extinction

ELECTROMAGNETISM Equivalence of electricity and magnetism. An electric current can induce magnetism, conversely a moving magnet can generate electricity. An electromagnet consists of wire coiled around a piece of iron.

ELECTRON A tiny particle that moves outside the nucleus of an atom. Each electron has a single negative electric charge.

ELEMENT A substance made up of atoms of the same type. It cannot be chemically broken down into simpler substances, but it can be combined with different elements to make compounds.

EVOLUTION Gradual changes in a species that occur over time and may result in new species.

EXPERIMENT A controlled test carried out to provide evidence for or against a scientific idea or theory.

EXTINCTION The dying out of a species or group of species.

FORCE A push or pull that can make an object move, turn, or stop it from moving, or change its speed or direction of movement.

FOSSIL The trace or remains of a plant or animal preserved in rock, amber, peat, or ice.

Force of gravity

GALAXY A collection of stars, planets, gas, and dust. Galaxies are classified by their shape into four main types: elliptical, spiral, barred spiral, and irregular. Our Galaxy (the Milky Way) is spiral shaped.

GAMMA RAYS A stream of very high-energy electromagnetic radiation similar to X-rays but with more energy and a shorter wavelength. Gamma rays are given off by some radioactive substances.

GENE The basic unit of inheritance. A gene is a section of a chromosome that is responsible for producing a particular substance in a cell.

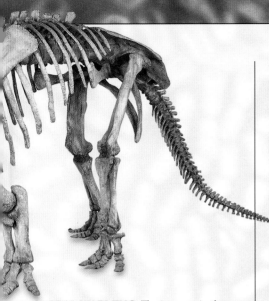

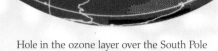

Hole in the ozone layer over the South Pole

GLOBAL WARMING The increase in the average temperature of the Earth's atmosphere.

GRAVITY The force that pulls objects together because of their masses. The weight of an object is equal to the force of gravity acting on it.

MAGNETISM The properties of attraction and repulsion that are shown by magnets. Every magnetic object has two poles, north and south. Two poles of the same type (north-north and south-south) repel each other whereas different poles (north-south) attract.

MASS The amount of matter in something. Mass is a basic property of an object, which stays the same even if gravity changes (unlike its weight, which changes according to gravity).

MICROORGANISM Also called a microbe, any organism that is so small it can be seen only with the aid of a microscope.

MOLECULE A group of atoms held together by chemical bonds. For example, a molecule of salt (sodium chloride) is made up of one sodium atom bonded to one chlorine atom.

NANOTECHNOLOGY The branch of technology concerned with making and manipulating objects and devices that are microscopically small (or even smaller). A nano is one-millionth of a millimeter.

NATURAL SELECTION The process by which organisms best adapted to their environment survive and those less well adapted are eliminated.

NEBULA A cloud of dust and gas in a galaxy. It is also used to describe any object in the night sky that appears as a fuzzy haze through a telescope.

NEUTRON A tiny particle that forms part of the nucleus of an atom; the other type

Water-filled glass acting as a prism

of particle in the nucleus is the proton. A neutron has no electric charge.

NUCLEAR FISSION The splitting of the nucleus of a large, heavy atom into smaller, lighter atoms. This process can produce large amounts of energy and radiation.

NUCLEUS In chemistry and physics this is the central part of an atom. It consists of one or more protons and one or more neutrons (except in hydrogen, which has only one proton and no neutrons). In biology, this is the central part of a cell that contains chromosomes.

ORBIT In astronomy, the path of one celestial object (or artificial satellite) around another; for example, the Moon's orbit is the path it follows circling the Earth. In physics, it is used to refer to the path of electrons around the nucleus of an atom.

OXYGEN A colorless, odorless gas that is essential for the life of most organisms. It makes up about one-fifth of the air in the Earth's atmosphere.

OZONE A form of oxygen. The ozone layer in the atmosphere helps block harmful ultraviolet light from the Sun.

PARTICLE A minute bit of matter. The word "particle" is often used to mean a subatomic particle such as an electron or neutron.

PASTEURIZATION The process of heating foods or liquids to destroy disease-causing organisms such as bacteria.

PLATE TECTONICS The theory that the Earth's crust is divided into large plates that move slowly.

PRISM An optical prism is a transparent object that can split light into its colors.

PROTON A tiny particle that forms part of the nucleus of an atom; the other type of particle in the nucleus is the neutron. A proton has a single positive charge.

PULLEY A simple machine consisting of a rope and one or more pulley wheels.

RADIATION Energy that travels in the form of electromagnetic waves, such as visible light, radio waves, ultraviolet light, infrared radiation, X-rays, and gamma rays. The word "radiation" is also used to refer to particles and rays given off during radioactive decay.

RADIOACTIVITY The emission (giving off) of particles or gamma rays that occurs when the nuclei of some heavy elements (such as uranium and plutonium) break down.

REFRACTION The bending of light when it passes through transparent material.

SCIENTIFIC LAW A statement about an event or phenomenon in nature that aims to describe what happens.

SEISMOMETER An instrument for measuring earthquakes.

SOLAR SYSTEM The Sun and the astronomical bodies that move around it. The solar system includes not only the major planets (such as the Earth) but also their moons and the asteroids, comets, and meteors.

SPECTRUM The array of colors produced when white light is split into its constituent wavelengths. A rainbow is an example of a natural spectrum produced when sunlight is split by raindrops. Can also refer to invisible emission of radiation, for example, X-rays.

STATISTICS The branch of mathematics that deals with the collection and analysis of numerical information.

THEORY An idea or principle put forward as a possible explanation for a set of facts or observations. A theory is tested by experiments to determine whether or not it is valid.

VACCINE A substance providing immunity to a disease-causing microorganism.

VERTEBRATE Any animal that has a spine (including humans and other mammals, birds, reptiles, and fish).

VIRUS A minute disease-causing agent that only reproduces inside living cells.

WAVELENGTH The distance between the crest of one wave and the crest of the next one. Used to describe frequency of light, electricity, magnetism, and sound.

X-RAYS High-energy electromagnetic radiation with a short wavelength. X-rays are widely used in medicine to produce images of the body's internal structures, especially bones.

Index

Acknowledgments

Dorling Kindersley would like to thank: Hilary Bird for the index; Dawn Bates for proofreading; Claire Bowers, David Ekholm-JAlbum, Sunita Gahir, Marie Greenwood, Joanne Little, Susan St. Louis, Steve Setford, and Bulent Yusef for the clip art; David Ball, Kathy Fahey, Neville Graham, Rose Horridge, Joanne Little, and Sue Nicholson for the wall chart; Margaret Parrish for Americanization.

The publishers would also like to thank the following for their kind permission to reproduce their photographs:

a-above; b-below/bottom; c-center; f-far; l-left; r-right; t-top

akg-images: 22cl, 26bl, 48cl, 52tc; Bibliothèque Nationale 14tl; Bibliothèque Nationale /VISIOARS 10c; Erich Lessing 16tl; Gerhard Ruf 14tr; Schütze / Rodemann 14clb; Alamy Images: archivberlin Fotoagentur GmbH 11cr; Sandra Baker 26–27bc; Scott Camazine 39cl, 46–47b; Nick Cobbling 62bl; Dennis Cox 10bc; Mary Evans Picture Library 1, 7br, 24tl, 34tl, 36bl, 42c, 42tl, 43tl, 69cra; eye35.com 15br; David R. Frazier Photolibrary, Inc. 56bl; Stephen Harrison 26–27bc (Lightning); ImageState 60bl; INTERFOTO Pressebildagentur 33cr; Martin Jenkinson 45br; kolvenbach 63br; Steve Mansfield-Devine 57bl; North Wind Picture Archives 17tr; PCL 6c; Popperfoto 32tl, 43cr; The Print Collector 7c, 9tl, 13cr, 41tr; QCumber 38cl; Ruby 61tl; Trip 12tl; Visual Arts Library (London) 18tr; Visual Arts Library (London) 6tl, 6br, 8tl, 12bc, 18tl, 19tr, 21b, 23br, 25br, 26tr, 27tc, 29tr, 30tl, 38tl; The Art Archive: 54tc; Musée des Beaux Arts Grenoble / Dagli Orti 24ca; Musée du Louvre Paris / Dagli Orti 13br; Private Collection / Marc Charmet 25tc; University Library Istanbul / Dagli Orti 12br; The Bridgeman Art Library: 39bl; British Museum, London 35cr; Down House, Kent 33br; Institut de Radium, Paris / Archives Charmet 43tr; Louvre, Paris, France / Peter Willi 17tr; Musée Conde, Chantilly, France/ Lauros / Giraudon

15c; Musée Pasteur, Institut Pasteur, Paris / Archives Charmet 39tc; Private Collection 9c, 28c; Private Collection / The Stapleton Collection 59c; Private Collection © Agnew's, London 28tr; Private Collection / Philip Mould, Historical Portraits Ltd, London 22tl; Warner Fabrics plc., Braintree, Essex 59clb; © CERN, Geneva: 69br; Corbis: 27br, 37l, 55tc; Theo Allofs / Zefa 62tr; Archivo Iconografico, S.A. 9br, 15tr; Lester V. Bergman 38clb; Bettmann 8c, 31tl, 44tl, 46tr, 47cr, 49tr, 55cla; epa 47cra; Shelley Gazin 60tl; Historical Picture Archive 16tl; Hulton-Deutsch Collection 43br, 44c; Matthias Kulka 63tr; Danny Lehman 60br; William Perlman / Star Ledger 33ca; Louie Psihoyos 55bl; Steve Raymer 40br; Roger Ressmeyer 50bc; Visuals Unlimited 59tc; DK Images: The British Museum 64tl; Tina Chambers / Courtesy of the National Maritime Museum, London 22br; Andy Crawford / Courtesy of David Ward 40crb; Andy Crawford / Courtesy of the Royal Museum of Scotland, Edinburgh 2bl, 12cr; Andy Crawford / Courtesy of the Royal Tyrrell Museum of Palaeontology, Alberta, Canada 71tl; Andy Crawford / Courtesy of the State Museum of Nature, Stuttgart 67br; Geoff Dann / Courtesy of the Imperial War Museum, London 54–55c; Geoff Dann / Courtesy of The Science Museum, London 57cla; Courtesy of Darwin Collection, The Home of Charles Darwin, Down House (English Heritage) 32cb; David Exton / The Science Museum, London 19crb; Neil Fletcher / Oxford University Museum of Natural History 30cra; Nelson Hancock / Rough Guides 37bl; Colin Keates / Courtesy of the Natural History Museum, London 24b (Carbon), 58c (Rose Quartz); Alan Keohane / Courtesy of the Arizona Mining and Mineral Museum, Phoenix 58c (Azurite & Malachite); Dave King / Courtesy of Down House / Natural History Museum, London 2br, 32ca, 32cr, 32c, 33bl, 33bc; Dave King / Courtesy of the Booth Museum of Natural History, Brighton 4cl, 31tr; Dave King / Courtesy of the Science Museum, London 3bc, 16bc, 20br, 21cla, 23t, 23cl,

34ca, 37cl, 37c; John Lepine / The Science Museum, London 10tl, 10–11c, 11ca; Andrew Leyerle / Courtesy of the Museum of Science and Industry, Chicago 67bl; NASA 11t, 47tl; NASA / Finley Holiday Films 17br, 65bl; Courtesy of the National Maritime Museum, London 48bc; Courtesy of the Natural History Museum, London 29br; Andrew Nelmerm / Courtesy of the Royal British Columbia Museum, Victoria, Canada 31bl; Liberto Perugi / Courtesy of the Museum of Natural History of the University of Florence, Zoology section 'La Specola' 18br; The Science Museum, London 2tl, 34–35bc; James Stevenson / Courtesy of the National Maritime Museum, London 29tl; Clive Streeter / Courtesy of The Science Museum, London 4tr, 9tr, 17tl, 21cra, 22bl, 24cb, 25clb, 26cr, 26br, 27tr, 36cl, 36br, 41tl, 42crb, 45cr, 65tc, 69c; Clive Streeter / Peter Griffiths - Modelmaker 51br; Harry Taylor / Courtesy of the Natural History Museum, London 30cb, 30cl, 41cl; Francesca Yorke / Courtesy of the Bradbury Science Museum, Los Alamos 47bc; European Space Agency: R. Gendler 50–51c; Flickr.com: 26c; Rob Francis: 31br; Getty Images: Alfred Eisenstaedt / Time Life Pictures 56clb; J.R. Eyerman / Time Life Pictures 50c; Hulton Archive 55cra; Imagno 48ca; Pascal Le Segretain 68b; Donald Uhrbrock / Time Life Pictures 56ca; NASA: The Hubble Heritage Team (AURA / STScI) 51tl; NSSDC 57c; The Natural History Museum, London: 20tl, 28–29c, 33tl; NOAO/AURA/NSF: 51tl, 51tc; Nobel Foundation: 68cla; Science & Society Picture Library: 17cla, 19c, 21ca, 25cra, 34cb, 35tl, 35tr, 35cb, 46c, 55c, 57tl, 58bl, 58–59c; Bletchley Park Trust 54c; NMPFT Associated Press 46bl; NMPFT Daily Herald Archive 58tl; Science Museum Archive 40tl; Science Photo Library: 20cl, 35br, 53cr, 58clb; A. Barrington Brown 52cl; Harvard College Observatory 50clb; Anthony Howarth 56cr; Peter Menzel 53bc; NASA 57tc, 57tr; C. Powell, P. Fowler & D. Perkins 43bl; Space Island Group: 62bl; Still Pictures: PHONE Labat Jean-Michel 7tr; The Wellcome Institute

Library, London: 39br, 42bc; Wikipedia, The Free Encyclopedia: 20bl.

Wall chart: akg-images: Erich Lessing (Galileo). Alamy Images: Mary Evans Picture Library (Babbage) (X-Ray); Mary Evans Picture Libary (Curie); North Wind Picture Archives (Edison); Popperfoto (Darwin); Visual Arts Library (London) (Aristotle) (Harvey) (Pasteur). The Bridgeman Art Library: Musée Pasteur, Institute Pasteur, Paris / Archives Charmet (Pasteur Miscoscope); Private Collection / Philip Mould, Historical Portraits Ltd, London (Newton). Corbis: (Kinetograph); Bettmann (Einstein); Historical Picture Archive (Faraday). DK Images: Courtesy of Down House / Natural History Museum, London (Darwin Notebook) (Darwin Beetles); Courtesy of The Science Museum, London (Telescope) (Edison Lamp) (Prism) (Zhang Heng) (Seismoscope) (Babbage Engine) (Faraday Experiment) (Periodic Table). European Space Agency: R. Gendler (Andromeda). Getty Images: Time Life Pictures / J.R. Eyerman (Hubble). Science Photo Library: A. Barrington Brown (Crick & Watson). Science & Society Picture Library: NMPFT Associated Press (Blackboard); Science Museum Archive (Mendeleyev).

Jacket images: Front: Alamy Images: Visual Arts Library (London) tr; Corbis: b: Historical Picture Archive cl; Getty Images: Joe McBride tl. Back: Alamy Images: Mary Evans Picture Library br; Corbis: fcl; DK Images: Courtesy the Science Museum, London cl; European Space Agency: R Gendler tc; Getty Images: Time & Life Pictures ftr; Mary Evans Picture Library: cb, fbr; Science Photo Library: Jean-Loup Charmet cr

All other images © Dorling Kindersley
For further information see: www.dkimages.com